Toproping

Rock Climbing
for the Outdoor Beginner

Second Edition

Bob Gaines

FALCONGUIDES

GUILFORD, CONNECTICUT

FALCONGUIDES®

An imprint of The Rowman & Littlefield Publishing Group, Inc.
4501 Forbes Blvd., Ste. 200
Lanham, MD 20706
www.rowman.com

Falcon and FalconGuides are registered trademarks and Make Adventure Your Story is a
trademark of The Rowman & Littlefield Publishing Group, Inc.

Distributed by NATIONAL BOOK NETWORK

British Library Cataloguing in Publication Information available

Library of Congress Cataloging-in-Publication Data

Names: Gaines, Bob, 1959– author.
Title: Toproping : rock climbing for the outdoor beginner / Bob Gaines.
Description: Second edition. | Guilford, Connecticut : FalconGuides, 2020.
    | Series: How to climb series | Includes index. | Summary: "Everything
    beginning climbers need to know to safely toprope climbing routes, from
    tying knots to setting anchors to belaying"— Provided by publisher.
Identifiers: LCCN 2019054451 (print) | LCCN 2019054452 (ebook) | ISBN
    9781493047819 (paperback) | ISBN 9781493047826 (epub)
Subjects: LCSH: Rock climbing.
Classification: LCC GV200.2 .G35 2020 (print) | LCC GV200.2 (ebook) | DDC
    796.522/3—dc23
LC record available at https://lccn.loc.gov/2019054451
LC ebook record available at https://lccn.loc.gov/2019054452

♾️™ The paper used in this publication meets the minimum requirements of American
National Standard for Information Sciences—Permanence of Paper for Printed Library
Materials, ANSI/NISO Z39.48-1992.

Contents

Chapter 7: Knots

137

Chapter 8: Belaying and Lowering

169

Chapter 9: Rappelling

197

Chapter 10: Teaching Rock Climbing in a Toprope Environment

211

Chapter 11: Risk Management

221

Chapter 12: Leave No Trace Ethics

229

Acknowledgments

First of all I'd like to thank John Burbidge at FalconGuides for putting it all together.

Thanks to Wills Young for his insights on face climbing techniques.

Thanks to the climbers who posed for photos: Calista Holden, Michael Bains, Patty Kline, Steve Schwartz, Frank Bentwood, Mike Morretti, Nicole Miyoshi, and Vivian Koo.

Thanks to the guides who posed while demonstrating techniques: Tony Sartin, Terri Condon, Peter Croft, Erik Kramer-Webb, Tony Grice, Erin Guinn, Jarad Stiles, Lisa Rands, Wills Young, Bryan Baez, Robin Depke, and Adam Radford.

Thanks also to my fellow guides and mentors, from whom I've learned a great deal: Chris Baumann, Jarad Stiles, Adam Fox, Jon Tierney, Alan Jolley, Peter Croft, Scott Cosgrove, Marcus Jollif, Todd Vogel, Erik Kramer-Webb, Tony Grice, Tony Sartin, Pat Dennis, and Dave Mayville.

Special thanks to John Long for the many insightful conversations we had while working on the *Climbing Anchors* books.

Thanks to my wife, Yvonne, for her help with the photography, and for being my number-one climbing partner.

Introduction

Toproping is the safest way to practice rock climbing techniques. For many enthusiasts it is the most enjoyable form of rock climbing. It's true that bouldering, with its inherent simplicity, is less complicated than toproping, with a great sense of freedom of movement, unfettered by complicated gear and rigging—the only equipment needed is your shoes, chalk bag, and maybe a crash pad with a buddy to spot you while you push your limits in a relatively safe environment. But bouldering is very limiting in another way: The higher you climb above the ground, the scarier it gets. And one thing is certain: When you fall, you hit the ground. Hitting the crash pad from 10 feet off the ground can be a bone-jarring experience. Many of my fellow climbers sustained the most serious injuries of their entire climbing careers because of a fall while bouldering.

Lead climbing is challenging both physically and mentally—figuring out not only the moves but also the complexities of protection placements along the way. The mental focus required to lead difficult trad (traditional) routes is intense, including the psychological aspect that comes into play when you move high above your protection, risking a long leader fall. Sport climbing is less demanding psychologically, allowing you to push physical boundaries, but stopping and clipping a long series of bolts interrupts the purity of the flow.

Free soloing has been said to be the purest form of rock climbing, but there is a fine line between the pure joy of fun-in-the-sun rock climbing, moving and flowing up the climb with nothing but air beneath your feet, and the sudden shadow of fear that can take over as quickly as a dark cloud eclipsing the sun. The free soloist faces the possibility of the ultimate irony: falling and dying as a direct result of being afraid to die, knowingly risking life for the pleasure of pure, unfettered freedom of movement.

So for many, toproping is the most relaxing form of rock climbing, and definitely the safest. With the practice of sound safety fundamentals, the toprope climber, free from the psychological fear of falling, uninterrupted from any need to place or clip protection, can achieve a Zen-like purity of focused movement rarely attained in the other forms of rock climbing. For the novice, toproping is the best and safest way to practice technique—unlike bouldering, where falls can be sudden and off-balance because knowing when a fall is imminent has not yet become instinctive. Once you learn the fundamentals of knots, anchoring, and belaying, toprope climbing is the best and safest method to quickly hone technique without the risk of potentially injurious falls.

This book is written from an instructor's perspective. For more than thirty-five years, I've worked as a professional climbing guide and manager of a rock climbing school, working in a toprope environment. Many of the techniques in this book were learned over these years. From every guide I've worked with along the way, I've gleaned some modicum of knowledge. In recent years I've received training from some of the top mentors in the country through the American Mountain Guides Association, discussing techniques for teaching rock climbing in a toprope setting and staying current with state-of-the-art methods. I'm currently an instructor for the AMGA's Single Pitch Instructor Course, and many of the principles in this book are a result of my exposure to and collaboration with other instructors.

For the beginner, this book will give you all the information you need to get started. For the intermediate climber, this book will refresh your knowledge on key concepts as well as teach you some new ones. For the experienced climber, this book will reinforce fundamentals and give you some new methods for rigging topropes.

Whether you are taking a few friends or family members out climbing or teaching a group of clients as a professional, the responsibility of a safe outing is in your hands. The fundamentals of safe rigging and risk management are the same whether or not you are a professional. My goal in this book is to pass along some of the things I've learned from experience: what to watch out for, and how to streamline the rigging of safe toprope anchor systems.

After you've mastered the skills in this book and are ready to progress to lead climbing and multi-pitch climbing, my book *Advanced Rock Climbing* covers these topics and much more.

Toproping is the safest way to practice technique and build confidence.

Getting Started

Site Selection

The ideal toprope crag is less than 100 feet high, with an aesthetic, sheer face of rock. It offers an easy walk to the top of the cliff; bomber anchors; clean, solid rock that minimizes rockfall danger; and a flat, comfortable base for belaying and hanging out. The perfect cliff has numerous routes at the level you find enjoyable and challenging for a fun day at the crag. To find your ideal crag, consult a climbing guidebook or ask for recommendations at your local climbing retail shop.

Guidebooks and Ratings

Guidebooks will usually give you a description of how difficult it is to approach and descend from a particular cliff, along with a description of the location and rating of the routes on the cliff. Most guidebooks include topos—either a photo of the cliff with the route lines marked, along with a verbal description, or a diagram of the routes with the route lines marked and symbols identifying the location of features like cracks, corners, chimneys, trees, bolts, fixed rappel anchors, etc. Studying a

A topo is a photo or other diagram detailing the location of the routes on a particular cliff.

Toproping at Joshua Tree National Park, California

guidebook's description can tell you if the top of a particular cliff can be easily approached and descended without any Class 4 or 5 climbing. Well-known toproping cliffs are usually popular because they have easy access, good anchors, and good-quality climbs.

This is the Class 1–5 rating system:

Class 1: Walking on relatively flat ground and trail hiking

Class 2: Hiking over rough ground, such as scree and talus; may include the use of hands for stability

Class 3: Scrambling that requires the use of hands and careful foot placement

A Typical Day of Toproping

John and Jill had done their homework and studied the guidebook before they arrived at their crag of choice. From the parking area it was just a short hike to the crag. It was a fine spring day, sunny but cool, and as luck would have it, they had the crag all to themselves. Jill pulled the guidebook out of her pack and surveyed the rock face.

"It says the approach to the top is Class 3 over on the north side. Let's gear up here. There are a bunch of routes we can set up!"

They put on their harnesses and sorted their rack. Between them they had two sets of cams to 3 inches, plus a good selection of nuts, carabiners, and slings, two cordelettes, a 100-foot low-stretch rigging rope, and a 60-meter dynamic climbing rope. They both were wearing approach shoes with sticky rubber, which gave them confidence in their footing for the short but exposed scramble to the top.

"Let's set up the 5.6 to warm up," John said.

They built two separate anchors—each with three cams equalized with a cordelette—and then used their extension rope, configured in the Joshua Tree System, to extend the rigging over the edge of the cliff so that the climbing rope would not be running over a sharp edge that could cause wear or even cut it. They each used a double-length nylon sling, attached to one leg of the rigging rope with a klemheist knot, connected to the belay loop on their harness with a locking carabiner, to protect themselves as they approached the edge. They each rappelled down by pre-rigging their ATC (Air Traffic Controller) rappel devices onto the climbing rope, backed up with an autoblock knot.

When they were both back down at the base, Jill built a ground anchor by slinging a tunnel between two boulders. Since John outweighed her by 100 pounds, she'd learned to always anchor herself when belaying him so she wouldn't get pulled from her stance if he fell. She tied into the end of the rope and connected herself to the ground anchor with a clove hitch, a knot that allowed her to easily adjust the length of the anchor rope. They checked each other's harness buckles and knots, a safety ritual they always went through before every climb.

"On belay?" John asked.

"Belay on," Jill responded.

"Climbing," John said.

"Climb on," Jill responded. These well-practiced commands were standard on all their climbs and allowed them to make absolutely certain that each knew what the other person was doing.

Class 4: Scrambling over steep and exposed terrain; a rope may be used for safety on exposed areas

Class 5: Technical "free" climbing where terrain is steep and exposed, requiring the use of ropes, protection hardware, and related techniques; *see Yosemite Decimal System (YDS)*

Class 6: Aid climbing where climbing equipment is used for balance, rest, or progress; denoted with a capital "A" followed by numerals "0" to "5" (e.g., 5.9/A3 means the free climbing difficulties are up to 5.9 with an aid section of A3 difficulty)

Jill belayed John while he did the climb. When he reached the top and was ready to be lowered, John yelled, "Tension."

"Tension on," Jill said as she pulled the rope tight to hold John's weight.

"Lower me," John said.

"Lowering," Jill said, and she slowly began to feed rope through her belay device while John "walked" down the climb in a sitting position with his feet out in front of him.

When he got to the ground, John said, "Off belay."

"Belay off," Jill said. She took the rope out of her belay device, untied from the ground anchor, and got ready to climb.

They both did the climb twice, and when Jill reached the top the second time, she topped-out to rig another climb. "Off belay," she called to John after she was safe. "Belay off" was John's response after he had unclipped the rope from his belay device.

Jill rigged another anchor on the highest part of the cliff directly above the next climb they wanted to toprope, a steep and intimidating 5.8 crack. Her anchor consisted of four cams in two separate cracks, equalized to a master point with slings and a cordelette. To safeguard herself while building the anchor, Jill had clipped into what she considered her best cam with a sling attached to her harness. She backed up her rappel device with an autoblock. She had John tie knots in the ends of her rappel rope to close the system, a habit they always used while rappelling or toproping in a single-pitch scenario.

Jill knew the climb would be right at John's limit of difficulty (crack climbs were not his forte), so she placed a cam for a ground anchor and belayed him with the Grigri, anticipating that he might need to hang and rest. Sure enough, halfway up the crack John's forearms were pumped and he was struggling.

"Tension!" he yelled.

"Tension on," Jill responded, and since she was belaying with the Grigri and was tight to her ground anchor, it was easy to hold his weight. "I've got you," she said. "Take your time and rest up; it's no problem to hold you." After he hung for a few minutes, John said he was ready to climb again.

"You got this!" Jill encouraged. John finished the climb and lowered down, a bit discouraged.

Jill waltzed up the crack, looking fairly relaxed. "You made it look easy," John said.

"Easy on a toprope" was Jill's response. "I don't know if I could lead that. Stopping to place protection would take a lot more energy."

Continued on next page

The Yosemite Decimal System

If you travel to foreign countries to go rock climbing, you'll notice that every country seems to have its own rating system, which can be a bit confusing. In American rock climbing we use what is known as the Yosemite Decimal System (YDS), which rates Class 5 climbs based on the most difficult section of the climb, called the crux, on a scale from 5.0 to 5.15. A climb graded 5.0 to 5.5 is usually appropriate for beginners, a climb rated from 5.6 to 5.9 is considered intermediate level, and a climb graded 5.10 and higher is in the realm of experts and experienced climbers. The "rating" of a climb is such an abstract concept that to get a sense of what it really means, you need to get on the rock and experience a wide variety of techniques. For example, a low-angle slab that is as smooth as a pane of glass can be rated the same as a big overhang with doorknob-size handholds.

The YDS was actually first developed in the 1950s at Tahquitz Rock, a 1,000-foot-high dome of granite that rises from a mountainside high above

Continued from previous page

They took a break for lunch and scoped out some impressive face climbs on the right side of the cliff. "From the bolt anchor we can toprope the 5.9 and the 5.10a off the same anchor if we use a directional," John said.

"Great idea," said Jill. "A two for one deal!"

John climbed the crack again, this time without falling or hanging on the rope, a small victory for him. After he reached the anchor he clipped in with a sling, then yelled, "Off belay, Jill!" and de-rigged the anchor.

He walked over to the 2-bolt anchor and decided to rig it using a cordelette and a self-equalizing "quad" rig, knowing that the direction of pull would change for each of the two climbs and the quad is a perfect anchor rig for that situation. One climb was directly below the anchor; the other started about 15 feet to the right. That climb would require a "directional," meaning the rope would have to run through a piece of protection to keep it above the climb and prevent the climber from swinging if a fall occurred. John tied stopper knots in both ends of the rope before tossing it down—the climb was nearly 100 feet high (half his rope length), and the side directional would make the rope even shorter. He rigged an autoblock backup for his rappel, allowing him to go hands-free as he set the directional anchor (two cams equalized with a sliding X) in a crack about 20 feet down and 15 feet right of his quad anchor.

Jill and John climbed both routes twice. When Jill reached the anchor the final time, she decided to rappel down because the 2-bolt anchor was equipped with chains and metal rings and the downclimb looked a little tricky. Before she went off belay, she took a sling, girth-hitched it to her harness, and clipped into both of the rings with a locking carabiner as a safety. After telling John she was off belay, she threaded the rope through both rings, tying a stopper knot on the end she just untied from, and checked to make sure John left a knot in the other end. Then she rappelled down to the base. Once on the ground she made sure the stopper knot was untied from one end of the rope before pulling down on the other end to retrieve the rope. She warned John when the end was almost through the anchor: "Heads up, John, rope coming down . . . ROPE!" so that John could move out of the way and not get whipped by the rope end. Jill coiled the rope and John reracked the gear. They packed up and made the short hike back to the parking area. At the car Jill pulled out a couple of cold drinks from a small cooler and handed one to John. "Here's to a great day of toproping," she said. "Cheers!"

Sticky rubber–soled approach shoes are indispensable for Class 2 and 3 terrain typically encountered while hiking to and from the crag.

the town of Idyllwild, in Southern California. In the 1940s and 1950s, local climbers often climbed their favorite Class 5 routes over and over again, rating them easy, moderate, or difficult Class 5. Eventually, when more routes were developed at Tahquitz, the climbers subdivided them into a scale of difficulty from 5.0 to 5.9. In 1952 Royal Robbins climbed the first 5.9 route in America when he made the first free ascent (i.e., without resorting to hanging on gear for aid or rest) of Tahquitz Rock's Open Book route. It wasn't until the 1960s that the first 5.10 routes were climbed in America, at Yosemite. It was here in Yosemite Valley that the YDS rating system was refined, and eventually the 5.11 and 5.12 grades were added. Today the most difficult climbs in the world are rated 5.15, and it's only a matter of time before someone climbs a 5.16.

One refinement of the YDS is that above 5.9 the grades are even further subdivided into four letter grades: a, b, c, and d, starting with 5.10a. For example, a 5.10d is the most difficult 5.10, and a 5.11a is the easiest 5.11.

Ratings are subjective, abstract concepts and will seem right or wrong depending on your height, skill level, and other factors like temperature, the condition of your climbing shoes, and how much you drank the night before. The rating of a particular route is assigned by the first ascent party, who also gets the honor of naming the route. A "sandbag" rating is an underrated climb, done so usually for egotistical reasons. With today's social media, climbing websites often allow for everyone's opinion on a climb's rating, so the process has become more democratic, and guidebook authors will often change the rating of a climb due to general consensus.

The Big Picture

To understand where toproping fits into the grand scheme of things, you should understand the various types of climbing situations. Use the glossary in the back of this book to look up any undefined terms referenced in the text, as many of the techniques used in other types of climbing, like leading and multi-pitch climbing, are not covered in depth in this book. But to get things started, here's a breakdown of the main categories and subcategories of rock climbing.

Perhaps the simplest form of rock climbing is **bouldering**—climbing small rock faces and boulders without the use of any equipment other than climbing shoes and a chalk bag. A fall while bouldering guarantees you'll hit the ground, so many practitioners use a crash pad specifically designed for bouldering, along with a partner or two to spot them and help them land safely. The role of a spotter is not to physically catch a falling climber but to assist him, like in gymnastics, directing him with outstretched arms to help him land (hopefully) on his feet and in balance.

Toproping is climbing with the use of a top anchor, typically on a cliff less than 100 feet high, with the rope running through a toprope anchor rigged at the top of the cliff. The climber is tied into one end of the rope, which goes up through the anchor and back down to the belayer. As the climber ascends the route, the belayer manages the slack, and is ready to hold the weight of the climber if he should fall. When the climber reaches the anchor, he is typically lowered back down to the ground by the belayer. Another toprope scenario is when the belayer belays from the top of the cliff as the climber ascends from below.

Leading is when a climber ties in to the end of the rope and climbs up the cliff, trailing the rope below her, with the belayer paying out rope as the leader climbs. The leader places **protection** (or pro) and clips the rope into the gear as she proceeds. If the leader falls (and the protection holds), she will fall at least twice the distance above the last piece of protection before the belayer can stop the fall. This is known as a **leader fall.** Once the climber reaches the end of the pitch (which can be only as long as the rope), she stops and builds a belay anchor, usually at a good ledge or stance. The second, or follower, cleans the gear as he climbs the pitch and reaches the belay anchor. If this is the top of the climb, it is called a one-pitch climb. A **pitch** is the distance between belay points. If the team proceeds higher, up another pitch, the climb becomes a multi-pitch climb. Big wall climbs in Yosemite, like those on El Capitan, have as many as thirty pitches.

Trad, or **traditional, climbing** is when gear (nuts, cams, etc.) is used for protection and anchors. Trad climbing can have some bolts thrown in the mix of protection and anchors, but involves mostly gear placements. **Sport climbing,** by definition, is an entirely bolted climb. No gear other than quick-draws (short slings with two carabiners attached for clipping bolts), a few slings, and carabiners is required, as the protection consists entirely of bolts, usually spaced no more than a body length or two, and the anchor is a bolted anchor.

Free climbing is climbing the rock with a rope for protection, but not hanging on the rope or the equipment for assistance on the actual ascent. **Aid climbing** is a form of ascent that uses gear to support the climber's weight and make upward progress. **Free soloing** is climbing without a rope.

CHAPTER TWO

Basic Equipment

Harness

I began climbing before the advent of the modern climbing harness. Instead of a harness, I used a swami belt. I took a 20-foot length of 2-inch-wide nylon webbing (rated at 8,000 lb.), wrapped it a bunch of times around my waist, and tied it with a water knot. Then I tied my climbing rope around the swami belt with a figure eight follow-through. This setup discouraged **hangdogging** and was rib jarring in a leader fall! Soon we figured out how to add leg loops, which made the rig more comfortable to say the least!

Harnesses have come a long way since the swami belt days. Look for a model that has a belay loop and gear loops. If you'll be climbing in different seasons, with differing clothing, a harness with adjustable leg loops is a good choice. Top brands include Arc'teryx, Black Diamond, Petzl, Metolius, Wild Country, Singing Rock, Trango, Mammut, and Camp USA. Most newer models have webbing with "speed buckles" that are pre-threaded and already doubled back, so all you have to do is loosen them before you put the harness on, then tighten the webbing to fit. Be aware that some harnesses have the old-school "double pass" buckle, where the webbing belt must be doubled back through the buckle. Check the manufacturer's guidelines on the

Modern, lightweight climbing harness

Basic equipment for toproping includes nuts, camming devices, carabiners, slings, and cordelettes.

Traditional, doubled-back buckle

Modern "speed buckle"

Harness with adjustable leg loops

harness you buy, and read the instructions on how to properly buckle and use the harness.

You'll want to retire your harness if the belay loop becomes frayed or shows signs of wear. Petzl recommends using nylon products no longer than seven years, even with minimal use.

Shoes

In the 1970s the EB was the best rock climbing shoe. The rubber wasn't very sticky, so most of the difficult routes during that era were done with precise and exacting edging technique. Around 1980 the first sticky rubber shoe of the modern era, called the Fire (pronounced "FEE-ray"), was sold by Boreal, and it revolutionized face climbing. Now most of the extreme slab routes can be done via smearing technique, and the extreme face climbs of the 1970s seem significantly easier. I can remember the first time I wore Fires, testing them out on the Camp 4 boulders in Yosemite. I was able to do many boulder problems I could never touch before, thanks to the magical smearing ability of the new rubber.

There are myriad styles and models of climbing shoes on the market today, all with very sticky rubber.

There will always be debate over which brand of rubber is the stickiest, but the gold standard for many years has been the Five Ten brand's "C4" rubber. If you ask a climbing shoe resoler which rubber is the most requested for use as a resole, no doubt the answer will be Five Ten C4.

For your first climbing shoe, choose a shoe that fits your foot the best and is comfortable. After you become obsessed with rock climbing, you'll probably own several shoes for different types of climbing. Top climbing shoe brands include Five Ten, La Sportiva, Mad Rock, Evolve, Butura, and Scarpa.

Selection of rock climbing shoes at Nomad Ventures climbing shop in Idyllwild, California

Chalk Bag

Once you start using chalk, you'll no doubt become hopelessly addicted (like I am). There is no question chalk will help provide a better grip, particularly on more difficult routes in warmer conditions. I like to use a chalk bag on a belt so that I can move it from side to side, or away from my back when I'm climbing wide cracks or chimneys. The Endo brand, distributed by Frank Endo, has always been my favorite. A soft brush (like a toothbrush) is useful for brushing away excess chalk and cleaning dirt off holds.

A chalk bag should have a belt so you can move it around your waist and a drawstring closure to keep the chalk from spilling out when you're not using it. Chalk is sold in small blocks that can be crushed into powder.

Helmets

Back in the 1960s and 1970s, very few climbers (less than 10 percent, I'd say) wore helmets. You were considered a geek and "not cool" if you wore a helmet. Today it's the opposite. Most climbers (probably around 80 percent) wear helmets, particularly in trad climbing areas.

Even in the seemingly benign toprope environment, hazards do exist. Rockfall can be a threat, especially if there is loose rock at the top of the cliff. Be especially aware when other climbers are at the top, rigging anchors and setting ropes, as rocks are easily dislodged by ropes being pulled around. When teaching groups, I always establish a mandatory helmet zone at the base of the cliff, and then watch for clients who are lounging at the base without a helmet.

If you are on the cliff or at the top of the cliff and dislodge a rock (or any object), the universal signal is "ROCK!" How loud the signal is yelled usually signifies the size of the rock. My closest calls in more than forty years of climbing have been with near-miss rockfalls. If the warning comes from 100 feet or more away, you may want to look up, judge the trajectory, and move aside accordingly. If the signal comes from just above you, and you haven't seen it happen, you might just want to hunker down and not look up, so as not to get hit in the face. Obviously, wearing a helmet is a good idea when climbing, belaying from the base of the climb, and hanging out at the bottom of the cliff.

Whether or not you choose to wear a helmet is up to you, but be aware that many fatal climbing incidents could have been prevented if the climber had been wearing a helmet. Rockfall, whether caused by other climbers, the rope, or natural causes, is always a danger. Top brands of climbing helmets include Petzl, Black Diamond, Mammut, and Camp USA.

A selection of modern climbing helmets from Nomad Ventures climbing shop, Joshua Tree, California

Rope

There are three basic types of ropes used in climbing: dynamic, low-stretch, and static. A dynamic rope is the most commonly used rope for toproping and lead climbing; it will stretch up to 25 to 35 percent during a leader fall and around 10 percent in a toprope fall. A low-stretch rope has relatively low stretch and therefore should not be used for lead climbing, because rope stretch is the key to absorbing the energy generated in a leader fall. A static rope, by definition, is just that—very low stretch. Think of it like a wire cable. Static ropes generally have very poor handling characteristics due to their stiffness and are typically used for fixed lines, hauling, and rappelling, where dynamic properties are not required.

Rope stretch is one of the hazards inherent in a toprope situation. Modern dynamic ropes stretch approximately 8 or 9 percent under body weight (just hanging your weight on the rope, called "static elongation") and a bit more in a fall with a touch of slack in the rope ("dynamic elongation"). Picture a 100-foot-high cliff set up as a toprope using a dynamic rope. At the start of the climb, you'll have 200 feet of rope in the system.

Let's say you're belaying a climber, with a bit of slack, who falls 15 feet up the route. Do the math: 185 feet of rope times 10 percent stretch equals 18.5 feet of rope stretch. Without you tightening the rope to take the slack out of the system, and tensioning the rope a bit to even further reduce the stretch, your climber will hit the ground, albeit with some deceleration as the stretch of the rope kicks in.

In my climbing school we've used low-stretch ropes (also called low-elongation or semi-static ropes) for our toproping classes for more than thirty-five years. These ropes stretch about 4 percent under body weight, slightly more in a toprope fall with a bit of slack. From a risk management standpoint, it just makes sense to use a low-stretch rope for toprope situations, especially if you're setting up relatively long routes (up to 100 feet high). The characteristics I look for in a low-stretch rope are EN 1891 certification, Type A designation, elongation in the 3 to 4 percent range under body weight, and a suppleness that tells you the rope will hold knots firmly and handle well for belaying. Sterling makes an excellent low-stretch rope called the Safety Pro. I prefer the 10mm diameter for good handling and durability.

Selection of ropes at Nomad Ventures climbing shop, Idyllwild, California

With technological advancements in rope manufacturing, modern "static" ropes stretch hardly at all, some as little as 1 percent under body weight. These ropes should not be used for toprope belaying but can be used for anchor rigging, although I also prefer a low-stretch for that application.

If using a dynamic rope for toprope belaying, beware of the dangers of rope stretch, and keep the rope taut in situations where the climber is just off the ground or just above a ledge.

A good choice for your first rope is a 60m × 10mm-diameter rope. You'll have a choice of a "dry coating" versus a "non-dry" rope. The dry coating is applied so the rope will not absorb water, which is

useful for alpine climbing and mountaineering and climbing in wet conditions, as a wet rope is weaker. Dry ropes are more expensive than non-dry ones. For pure rock climbing in dry conditions, save your money and buy a non-dry rope.

Recently there has been a trend toward ever-thinner ropes. Ropes as thin as 9.0mm in diameter are UIAA rated for lead climbing. But these thinner ropes are stretchier and will wear out far more quickly. For toproping I don't recommend going below 9.8mm in diameter for your climbing rope, and 10mm to 10.2mm diameter will be more durable in the long run.

Rope Care and Use

When buying a climbing rope, purchase it from a climbing shop that specializes in selling climbing gear. A dynamic climbing rope should have UIAA (Union Internationale des Associations d'Alpinisme) and/or CE (Certified for Europe) certification to EN (European Norm) 892. This means the rope has been tested and approved by a UIAA-approved testing facility. Static and low-stretch (or low-elongation) ropes are tested in Europe to meet EN 1891. In the United States, static and low-stretch ropes are tested by UL (Underwriters Laboratories) to meet NFPA 1983 (National Fire Protection Association Standard). Any reputable climbing shop will stock only the top brands, like Sterling, Maxim, Beal, Bluewater, Mammut, Edelrid, Edelweiss, Petzl, Millet, Metolius, and PMI.

Avoid setting up a toprope where your rope might abrade over an edge when someone is being lowered. This can severely weaken or ruin your sheath in just one climb/lower cycle! Avoid standing or stepping on your rope, as this can grind sharp pebbles and grit through the sheath and into the core. A tarp or rope bag is useful in areas where the base of the cliff is sandy or dirty. This will keep your rope neater and cleaner and prevent it from picking up silt and dirt that can wear out your carabiners and belay device faster. Minimize your rope's exposure to UV light, as this will weaken the fibers over time. Store your rope in a shaded, dry place.

If your rope gets dirty, you can wash it by hand in a tub, or in a washing machine (preferably a front-loading washing machine, because a top-loading machine's agitator will abrade the rope) with hot water and soap suitable for nylon. If washing your rope in a bathtub, make sure the tub is free of any chemicals that may damage it. I daisy-chain the full length of my rope before washing it in a machine to keep it from getting tangled. Let your rope dry by hanging it in a shaded area.

Be vigilant and protect your rope from coming into contact with any chemicals that contain acids, bleaching or oxidizing agents, and alkalines. Acid is the archenemy of nylon and can severely weaken nylon and polyester fibers. Be extremely careful to avoid exposing your rope to battery acid or any type of acid that may be encountered in your garage or the trunk of your car. Again, it is wise to keep and store your rope in a rope bag.

It is not a good idea to borrow or rent a rope, because you don't know its history. Don't lend out your rope, and keep track of its history and how long you've had it. Most manufacturers recommend keeping a rope for no longer than five to seven years even with minimal use, and no longer than ten years even if the rope has been stored and never used.

Inspect your rope by running your hand over the entire length of the sheath when coiling and uncoiling the rope. Visually inspect for excessively worn areas of the sheath, and feel for irregularities (voids, flat spots, etc.) in the core. Your rope should be retired (or cut to a shorter length) if you see the sheath is excessively worn or frayed, exposing the core, or if there are any anomalies in the core.

Marking the Middle of Your Rope

Many climbers use a black felt-tip marking pen to mark the midpoint of their rope. In 2002 the UIAA Safety Commission issued a warning based on testing done by the UIAA and by some rope manufacturers that showed the ink from some marking pens decreased the strength (more specifically, the rope's ability to hold repeated falls in accordance with the EN 892 testing standard) by as much as 50 percent. While this may seem a shocking figure, the UIAA president pointed out that "such a marked rope can only break in practice when the two or three centimeters, which are marked, are placed over a sharp rock edge when the rope is loaded by a fall." While this is a very remote possibility, you may want to consider other alternatives to identify the midpoint on your rope, or at least use only marking pens sold or recommended by the manufacturer of your rope.

In 2013 Bluewater commented on the marking pen controversy: "Marking pens are fine to use on ropes as long as they are water based laundry markers. Years ago solvent based markers were the norm. Some of the solvents used in these old pens could reduce the strength of the sheath strands marked. These days most pens are water based so this is not as much of an issue as in years past. We recommend a Sharpie 'rub a dub' laundry marking pen. Some manufacturers sell marking pens they are confident will not harm your rope."

PMI sells the Sanford Sharpie TEC Rope Marker, which they claim "is the only pen that is batch tested for 24 trace elements, making it the only pen you can really trust for marking your rope."

Tape is not a good option, as it can slide on the rope or, more likely, become gummy and stick in rappel and belay devices. A good option, and my personal choice, is to buy a "bi-pattern" rope, which is a rope that changes pattern at the middle of the rope, without a change in yarns or color. Another option is a bicolor rope, which has a color change at the midpoint of the rope. The rope manufacturer changes yarns and joins the yarns together with what is known as an "air splice" (forcing the ends to entwine around each other using extremely high air pressure). The process creates a cosmetic blemish at the yarn change, which the manufacturers say is actually stronger than continuous fibers because of the extra fibers at the splice. I've never been a fan, however, as cosmetically it looks questionable, and I've found the join to be a wear point because the fibers bulge slightly. If you don't have a middle mark on your rope, simply start with both ends and flake the rope out until you reach the middle.

Coiling and Uncoiling Your Rope

When you buy a new rope, take extra care the first time you uncoil it to prevent kinking. The Sterling Rope company recommends the following method. Start with one end and uncoil a few strands. Then go to the other end and uncoil a few strands. Go back and forth until the entire rope is uncoiled, then inspect the rope by running it through your hands (flaking it in a loose pile) from one end to the other. Another method is to simply unroll the rope from the coil, as if pulling it off a spool, holding the rope and rotating the coil until the entire rope is stacked on the ground, keeping the rope free from any twists, then coil it with the butterfly coil method after inspection.

THE BACKPACKER OR BUTTERFLY COIL

For toproping the best way to coil your rope is to use the butterfly, or backpacker, coil. This coiling method puts fewer kinks in your rope. It is also the fastest way to coil a rope, since you start with both ends and coil a doubled rope. I start by measuring two and a half arm lengths (both arms extended), then begin the butterfly. Finish it off by tying the

In situations where you'll need to scramble, the backpacker coil is an excellent way to carry your rope.

rope ends with a square knot around your waist. When you're ready to set up your toprope climb, start by flaking out the rope from the ends—you'll come to the middle of the rope when you're done flaking it out. Now you can clip the middle of the rope into your anchor, toss the ends down, and your toprope climb is set up.

The Backpacker or Butterfly Coil

The Backpacker or Butterfly Coil

THE MOUNTAINEER'S COIL

Another standard coiling method is called the mountaineer's coil. This is a traditional method that makes for a classic, round coil that can be easily carried over the shoulder or strapped onto the top of a pack. The big disadvantage of the mountaineer's coil is that it must be uncoiled as it was coiled; otherwise it's easy to form a mess of slipknots that are time-consuming and frustrating to resolve. A neat mountaineer's coil is also difficult to achieve on a kinked rope. The key when flaking out a mountaineer's coil is to take your time and uncoil it one loop at a time.

The Mountaineer's Coil

NEW ENGLAND COIL

This coiling method butterflies the rope, but as a single strand, making it easier to flake out and much less likely to tangle than the mountaineer's coil.

New England Coil

Slings and Webbing

Nylon Webbing

In the 1960s and 1970s, 1-inch-wide tubular nylon webbing was the standard sling material, tied into a loop with a water knot or double fisherman's knot. Eventually, sewn slings with bartacked stitching came onto the market and were actually stronger than the same material tied with a knot. Sewn slings are not only stronger but also safer in that you don't have to worry about the knot loosening and coming untied. Today nylon slings are typically sold in $^{11}/_{16}$-inch width, bartacked into 24-inch or 48-inch loops with a rating of 22 kN (4946 lb.).

Climbing shops still sell 1-inch tubular nylon webbing from spools, cut to any length you wish. Be aware that these spools of webbing contain taped splices where the webbing ends have been joined together with masking tape. It seems impossible for

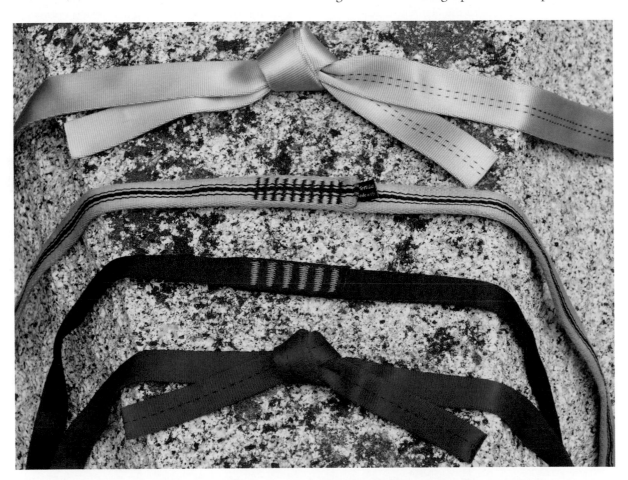

Nylon Sling Comparison. Top to bottom: 1-inch tubular nylon webbing tied with water knot (Sterling tech webbing, rated at 4,496 lb. tensile strength); 18 mm Metolius Nylon Sling, rated at 22 kN loop strength (4,946 lb.); 18 mm Black Diamond Nylon Runner, rated at 22 kN loop strength (4,946 lb.); $^{11}/_{16}$-inch Sterling tubular webbing, tied with water knot rated at 13 kN (3,000 lb.) tensile strength (straight pull on a single strand)

it to happen, but I know of two cases where spliced webbing was sold to customers who then used it with only the masking tape joining the webbing together, in one case with devastating results.

The Bluewater company recommends the maximum lifespan of its nylon webbing to be no more than five years and recommends retiring a nylon sling if it has been subjected to temperatures above 176°F, is scorched or glazed from a rope being pulled across it, shows signs of UV degradation from being left out in the elements (faded color and/or stiffness), or has been exposed to acid or bleach. Like nylon rope, nylon webbing can lose an appreciable amount of strength when wet or frozen. And remember, acid is the enemy of nylon. Keep your slings away from corrosive substances and solvents. Metolius warns: "Even fumes from a car battery can reduce the strength of your slings to the point they will fail under body weight."

For rigging and extending toprope anchors, a length of static or low-stretch rope (I prefer 10mm diameter) is far more versatile than webbing and is easier to tie knots with.

Spectra and Dyneema Slings

Spectra slings, introduced in the late 1980s, were lighter, less bulky, and stronger than nylon. Dyneema is a more recent innovation, typically sold in various-length loops sewn with bartacked stitching in 10mm width. Dyneema and Spectra both have almost the exact identical chemical makeup of high-molecular-weight polyethylene, which, pound for pound, is stronger than wire cable. Most experts say that the manufacturer of Dyneema consistently produces more high-quality fibers than the manufacturer of Spectra material, and most of the climbing slings on the market today are made from Dyneema.

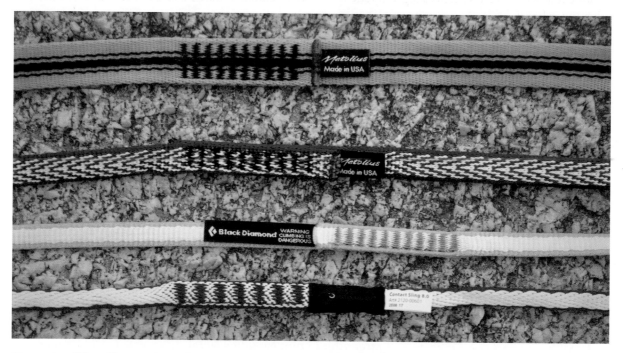

Dyneema Sling Comparison. Top to bottom: Metolius 18mm nylon sling (for comparison); Metolius 13mm Monster sling (nylon/Dyneema blend) (22kN/4,946 lb. loop strength); Black Diamond 10mm Dynex Runner (22 kN loop strength); Mammut 8mm Dyneema Contact Sling (22 kN loop strength)

Tensile Strength Versus Loop Strength

Strength ratings are often given as *tensile strength* and *loop strength*. Tensile strength is tested by a straight pull on a single strand of the material with no knots, done by wrapping the material around a smooth bar (4-inch diameter gives the most accurate test) on both ends and pulling until it breaks. Loop strength is the material tested in a loop configuration, either tied with a knot (in the case of webbing, usually the water knot) or sewn with bartacked stitching. In general, webbing loop strength when tied with a water knot is about 80 percent of twice the tensile breaking strength, and bartacked sewn webbing loop strength is generally about 15 percent stronger than the same material tied with a water knot, depending on the quality and number of bartacks.

Both Spectra and Dyneema slings are constructed from parallel fibers—very strong but with high lubricity, which means the material itself is inherently slick. That is the reason you can only buy it in sewn loops—it does not hold knots well. Do not cut a Spectra or Dyneema sling and retie it with a water knot!

Both Spectra and Dyneema have a lower melting point than nylon (around 285°F for Dyneema/Spectra compared to nylon's melting point of around 480°F). The lower melting point, along with the inherent slipperiness, make Spectra and Dyneema slings a poor choice for tying friction hitches like the prusik, klemheist, or autoblock, compared to 5mm or 6mm diameter nylon cord.

In a pinch, if you need to use a sling to tie a friction hitch, use a nylon one over a Dyneema sling, because heating up a Dyneema sling can weaken it. The newer, thinner (10mm) Dyneema slings will work for friction hitches, and they do possess some nylon in their construction, but if they start to slide on a rope when under load, the friction will generate heat, which could potentially weaken the sling.

Dyneema fibers do not retain dye and cannot be colored, so the fiber is distinctive in that it is always white. Manufacturers add a blend of nylon to Dyneema to make it more durable, usually in a distinctive border pattern.

When using Dyneema slings, think of them like a wire cable—they have almost no stretch. Avoid tying knots with them—it can be almost impossible to untie a simple overhand knot in the newer, thinner Dyneema after it has been seriously weighted. Wild Country warns that the material loses a hefty

Girth-hitching two Dyneema slings together can decrease their strength by 50 percent, but for most toproping situations this is not a concern since the loop strength is 5,000 lb. to begin with.

percentage of its strength (around 50 percent) when tied in a simple overhand knot or girth-hitch—a property that nylon does not possess. The best way to use a Dyneema sling is clipped to carabiners. If using them in a sling-to-sling configuration, either basket one sling over another or use a properly tied girth-hitch.

Using a Dyneema sling for a personal tether is a poor choice, since if you slip and suddenly weight it, the sling has almost zero stretch and can be jarring to your back. Nylon is a better choice because it has a modicum of stretch, albeit minimal in the short length of a sling, but at least it has some shock-absorbing stretch.

When buying slings for toproping, about a half-dozen single-length (24-inch) and two double-length (48-inch) slings will suffice for most situations. Double-length (48-inch) sewn nylon slings are handy for tethering into anchors and extending your rappel device away from your harness.

Recent studies show that dirty slings are weaker than clean ones. The Mammut company suggests that "to maintain the quality and safety of your slings, you need to clean them regularly." Mammut recommends to "clean soiled slings in hand-hot water with a small amount of mild detergent or in a delicates machine cycle up to 30 degrees centigrade (86 degrees Fahrenheit). Rinse in clear water. Leave to dry in shade."

Cord and Cordelettes

A good all-purpose cordelette is 7mm-diameter nylon cord, about an 18- to 20-foot length tied into a giant loop with a double fisherman's knot. I prefer a length that allows me to double the cordelette within the span of my outstretched arms. My favorite brand is Sterling, whose 7mm-diameter nylon cord is rated at 12.4 kN (2,788 lb.) tensile strength and tests over 5,000 pounds when tied into a loop with a double fisherman's knot.

Cordelettes made with a Dyneema core and nylon sheath have incredibly high strength and low

stretch. Pound for pound, Dyneema is stronger than steel (and is the material used in body armor for the military), but Dyneema loses an appreciable amount of strength when tied with knots. Because these cords are so light and strong, with less bulk to carry, they have become popular, especially for multi-pitch climbing. The Bluewater company markets the 5.5mm-diameter Titan Cord, with a Dyneema core and nylon sheath, rated at 13.7 kN (3,080 lb.). They say its "combination of high strength, low elongation, and light weight provides superior characteristics over other combinations. Dyneema does not lose significant strength with repetitive flexing and offers a huge increase in abrasion and cut resistance over other materials. BW Titan cord can be cut and sealed with a hot knife. We recommend a triple fisherman's knot for tying 5.5 Titan into loops."

In recent years "high-tenacity" cords have come onto the market, utilizing aramid fibers (namely Technora) for the core, with a nylon sheath. Aramid fiber has an exceptionally high breaking strength (stronger than Spectra or Dyneema) with low stretch and an extremely high melting point (900°F), making it difficult to cut and melt. The Sterling 5.9mm PowerCord has a Technora core and nylon sheath, with a tensile breaking strength of around 19 kN (4,271 lb.); the 5mm Tech Cord, sold by Maxim/New England Ropes, with a 100 percent Technora core and polyester sheath, rates at a whopping 4,700 pounds tensile strength. But studies have shown that with repeated flexing, aramid fibers break down more quickly (losing strength) than good old-fashioned nylon. In fact, one particular study showed that when one section of Technora fiber cord was loaded with a 40-pound weight and flexed 180 degrees over an edge 1,000 times, the material lost 50 percent of its strength, while nylon cord, in the same test, lost virtually no strength. Further research may be warranted. The big advantage of these cords is their high strength and low bulk, which is advantageous for situations like multi-pitch climbing.

If you use Dyneema- or Technora-core cords,

Cord Comparison. Top to bottom: Bluewater 5.5mm Titan Cord tied with triple fisherman's knot (Dyneema core/nylon sheath, tensile strength 13.7 kN/3,080 lb.); Sterling 5.9mm PowerCord (Technora core/nylon sheath, tensile strength 19 kN/4,271 lb.); Sterling 7mm Nylon Cordelette (nylon core/nylon sheath, tensile strength 12.4 kN/2,788 lb.)

loop strength tests show that a triple fisherman's knot tests slightly stronger than a double fisherman's knot for these materials. In nylon cord, tests reveal no difference in loop strength when tied with a double or triple fisherman's, so a double fisherman's is the standard knot for joining nylon cord. Consider replacing Technora core cordelettes more often with high use. Keep in mind that the price tag on the high-tech cords is roughly twice as much as nylon. The bottom line is this: For an all-purpose cordelette for toproping, you can't go wrong with old-school nylon—it doesn't lose as much strength as the high-tech cords when tied with knots and has more stretch, which allows it to absorb energy

better than the high-tech cords. A good choice is 7mm-diameter nylon cord.

To tie friction hitches like the prusik, klemheist, and autoblock, you'll want to use 5mm- or 6mm-diameter nylon cord (nylon core, nylon sheath). When buying this accessory cord, buy the softest, most pliable cord you can find. A stiff cord won't grip as well when used for friction hitches. Also, be aware of the difference between 5mm nylon accessory cord (typically rated at 5.2 kN/1,169 lb.) and 5.5mm high-tenacity cord, like Bluewater Titan cord, rated at 13.7 kN (3,080 lb.). You obviously would not want to use 5mm nylon accessory cord for your cordelette!

Carabiners

Carabiners are used primarily to attach various links (like slings and rope) together in the anchor or belay chain. Locking carabiners are used in critical applications and in conjunction with belay and rappel devices. Carabiners come in a variety of shapes: oval, D-shaped, and pear-shaped.

A basic carabiner is of aluminum alloy, with a spring-loaded gate on one side. The spine of the carabiner is the solid bar stock opposite the gate.

The small protrusion on one end of the gate is called the nose, and this visually tells you which way the gate opens. The basic design has a small pin on the gate that latches into a groove on the nose end. The preferable "keylock" design eliminates the pin, and the gate and bar come together in a machined notch. A wire-gate carabiner simply has a wire under tension serving as the gate, which provides a wider opening because of its slim mass and eliminates "gate flutter," the vibration of a solid gate during a fall or peak loading of the carabiner.

Carabiners

Carabiners come in a dazzling array of designs for various applications. Top row (left to right): asymmetrical D, regular D, oval, wire-gate D, bent-gate D. Bottom: pear-shaped locking. The most useful carabiners for toproping are ovals, Ds, and pear-shaped locking. Bent-gate carabiners are used primarily for sport climbing (attached to the rope-clipping end of a quickdraw).

Carabiners

Left, Wiregate carabiner

Two oval carabiners with the gates properly opposed and reversed

Three oval carabiners opposed and reversed at a toprope anchor master point

Carabiners

Two pear-shaped locking carabiners with the gates opposed and reversed at a toprope anchor master point

Locking carabiners (left to right): Petzl William Triac, Petzl William Ball Lock, Black Diamond Twistlock, Black Diamond Screwgate

For toproping, oval carabiners are useful for racking gear, and for use in sets of two or three for connecting the climbing rope to the toprope anchor master point. Because of their symmetry, the gates can be opposed and reversed and the carabiner configuration still retains its oval shape. Two opposed and reversed ovals can also be used in lieu of a locking carabiner at any critical junction in the anchor system in situations where you've run out of locking carabiners and need extra security at a key point.

Locking carabiners are used for critical links and applications where it is absolutely imperative that the carabiner gate stays closed, like on a rappel or belay device, at a critical link in the anchor system, or when attaching the belayer's climbing rope to the anchor.

D-shaped carabiners have the strongest configuration because when the carabiner is loaded on the major (long) axis, the weight naturally is loaded closest to the spine. For this reason a locking D is a good choice for a belay/rappel carabiner. A locking pear-shaped carabiner is useful for many applications because of its wide aperture on one side; it is a good carabiner to use with a Munter hitch. It is also a great carabiner to pair up for use at the toprope anchor master point. When you oppose and reverse two pear-shaped locking carabiners, the symmetry is maintained (unlike an asymmetrical D shape), and the climbing rope runs smoothly through the carabiners.

The most common locking carabiner is the screwgate. The screwgate locking carabiner is just that, a mechanism with a collar that screws shut

Carabiners

Every carabiner you buy should have the UIAA breaking strength ratings stamped on the spine.

Bad. Never load a carabiner in three directions as shown here.

over the nose of the carabiner. I like the Petzl designs that show a red stripe (red means danger!) when the gate is unlocked. Obviously, with a screwgate locking carabiner, you have to remember to lock it, and it's an important habit to always check your locking carabiners to make sure they are locked. Check them with a close visual inspection, and also by pressing on the gate (squeeze test) for an additional safety precaution.

If you are a bit absentminded, or catch yourself occasionally not locking your screwgate carabiner, you might want to buy an autolock, or twistlock, carabiner. The twistlock design has a spring-loaded gate that locks automatically, and there are several autolocking designs on the market that have even safer mechanisms that must be manipulated (like pushing the gate upward then twisting the gate

to lock it, or pressing a button then twisting open the gate), but some climbers find these difficult to use. Interestingly, for industrial workers in the vertical rope access environment (rappelling and rope ascending on the faces of dams, buildings, and bridges), OSHA standards require autolocking carabiners, as does the tree-trimming industry.

An important thing to remember with carabiners is that a carabiner is only about one-third as strong if it's loaded with the gate open. It's essential, therefore, to keep a few things in mind when using a carabiner:

- Always load the carabiner in the proper direction—on the major, or long, axis.

- Do not cross-load a carabiner (on the minor axis) or load it in three directions (called tri-axial loading).

Carabiners

Never load a carabiner over an edge—its strength is compromised, and if the gate is forced open, the carabiner loses two-thirds of its strength.

By extending with a sling, the carabiner is now properly loaded in the strongest configuration, with the load on the spine of the carabiner.

- Do not load a carabiner over an edge of rock—this can open the gate when the carabiner is loaded, and two-thirds of the carabiner's strength will be lost.

Retire a carabiner if it shows a groove from excessive rope wear, or if it has been dropped a lengthy distance down a rock face and shows any obvious deformity. If the gate is sticky, washing it with soap and water and using some graphite lubricant will usually take care of the problem.

In the professional realm, the industry standard for attaching the climbing rope to the toprope anchor master point is either two locking or three oval carabiners with the gates opposed and reversed. I've always preferred three ovals because of the symmetry and wide base they present for the climbing rope. If using two locking carabiners, pick a pair of pear-shaped (not D-shaped) lockers so the pairing is symmetrical when one is opposed and reversed. I've used three ovals for thousands of client days without incident. Simply oppose and reverse the outside carabiners to the middle one. The wide radius created by the three carabiners provides a stable platform for the rope and tends not to flip sideways as often as two locking, a situation that can pin the rope against the rock while lowering if the climber's (weighted) strand is on the outside, away from the rock.

If you do a lot of toproping, you'll see that aluminum carabiners actually wear rather quickly, developing noticeable grooves. When this happens, you should retire them. The worn-off aluminum particles also get on the rope and the belayer's hands. Using steel ovals solves both wear issues, as steel is far more durable and wears much more slowly than aluminum.

Three steel ovals with the gates opposed and reversed at a toprope anchor master point

CHAPTER THREE

Face Climbing Techniques

Slab Climbing

When I began rock climbing in the early 1970s, the infamous "Stonemasters" ruled the Southern California crag scene. At that time, American and British climbers were setting the standards, and the Stonemasters were doing some of the hardest rock climbs in the world. Entrance to their elite clique was direct: You had to flash Valhalla, a three-pitch route at Suicide Rock, perhaps the first 5.11 edging climb in America. Back then, the best shoes were hard-rubber PAs and RDs, both totally unsuitable for difficult edging and smearing routes like Valhalla. Not until EBs came along did the ranks of the Stonemasters grow, although only slightly.

Everything changed when sticky rubber shoes arrived. Precise edging was out, and smearing was in—pasting the ball of the foot directly onto the rock, letting the edge, crystal, or merest rugosity "bite" into the boot sole. Some climbers referred to this new technique as "smedging." Around 1980 the Boreal Fire (pronounced "FEE-ray") arrived, with a dramatically stickier rubber, and a slab renaissance ensued. Some of the old test pieces seemed a full grade easier in the new boots, and by 1985 almost every serious Suicide climber was a Stonemaster. I remember a slab boulder problem at the Camp 4 boulders in Yosemite that I had tried in vain hundreds of times but was able to do first try with my brand-new pair of Fires. Such is the part technology has played in slab climbing.

Gavin Bridgeman topropes Sig Alert (5.10b), Joshua Tree National Park, California.

Extreme onsight slab climbing requires quick thinking to unravel puzzling move combinations. Exacting footwork is essential, as is balance and relaxation under duress. Even the slightest quaking will send the boot skating away.

I like to work in two sets: handhold and footholds. First I scan the rock for the two best handholds. On edges I prefer the "crimp" grip (placing the thumb over the forefinger) for optimal power, digging the finger pads straight down onto the holds for the most positive purchase. On difficult slab routes, the edges will generally be tiny—as thin as razor blades and one or two finger pads wide.

When no obvious edges are apparent, simply digging the finger pads into the most roughly textured area will help. Any downward pressure on the fingers is taking weight off the feet, making it easier for them to stick on sketchy holds. This is the key to hard slab climbing: maintaining points of contact and letting go with the fingers of one hand only to quickly latch the next edge.

Many of the most extreme slab cruxes consist of sidepull combinations, pulling sideways on vertical edges with arms extended in an iron-cross position. On low-angle slabs, palming is often the key and helps keep the center of gravity over the feet. The idea is "nose over toes."

In my experience as a climbing instructor at Joshua Tree, a common client profile for guided climbing is a client with at least some gym

Nose over toes. Carmen Cendejas climbs Leap Erickson (5.10b), Joshua Tree.

all climbing technique, even crack climbing, this builds a foundation that carries over to all other climbing techniques.

Watch a world-class climber and the first thing you'll notice is his or her fluid, ultraprecise footwork. Clients often ask me, "How can I have smooth footwork?" What I tell them is this: The first thing to do is mentally focus on it from the second you step off the ground. The goal is "quiet feet." If you're tapping or dragging your foot up the rock, you'll hear it. Climb with your eyes. Never take your eyes off the hold until your foot is set precisely on the hold, and consciously think about the best positioning of your foot on the hold. Never look for another handhold until both feet are set. Slowing down your movement will help you focus on precision.

Edges, sharp crystals, and protruding rugosities are the most obvious smearing targets. On low-angle blank slabs, often what you're looking for is simply a ripple or dimple that's slightly less steep. There are many friction climbs at Joshua Tree that

experience but little or no outdoor experience on real rock. For this situation I typically start clients off on a slab, for several reasons. One is to get them used to "reading" the rock, looking for the subtleties and nuances of face holds, which can be tough for someone used to seeing colored holds on a gym wall. Another reason is that it begins the learning curve of valuable lessons on smearing: what will stick and what won't. Each move is a lesson and a positive building of trust and confidence in the ability of the shoe's rubber to adhere to the rock. On a slab bereft of any obvious hand- and footholds, the client is forced to trust the friction of the boots while learning the subtleties of body position and center of gravity. Since footwork is the key to

Basic smearing profile. The heel should be lower relative to the toe. Angle the position of your foot to best take advantage of the shape of the smear. In general, you'll want your heel pointed away from the rock, but let the angle and shape of the hold dictate the position of your foot.

are completely devoid of edges, climbed via a series of smears that resemble a miniature version of moguls on a ski run.

When things get steeper and the route has more defined edges, remember that you can use both the inside and outside edge of the shoe. The basic edging technique is for the level of the heel to be slightly higher than the toe.

To rest, if you're on a tiny stance big enough for only one foot, use your heel to stand on it, resting your toes, while you shake out the other foot. Then switch feet and do the same. Another resting technique on a two-foot stance is to bend your knees and balance against the wall with your knees.

On traverses, crossing inside with the opposite foot works best, using the outside edge portion of the shoe that's crossing through to smear with.

Peter Croft demonstrates how to rest on tiny edges—hips in, knees against the rock—on Solid Gold (5.10), Joshua Tree National Park.

Ankle flexion helps maintain maximum surface contact between the rubber and the rock. Always focus on shifting the center of gravity to directly over the foothold you're stepping up on. A slightly dynamic technique with the lower leg will help you shift your center of gravity most effectively: Once the upper foot is set, bend the knee of the lower leg slightly and push off the lower hold as you shift your center of gravity to the upper foothold. This won't work for super high steps where you're most extended, but it will work most all the time and is a

To rest on a slab, place your heel on the hold, then shake out your other foot.

key fundamental that makes slab moves far less tiring on the legs.

On extremes slabs (5.12 and harder), where only the tiniest of edges, slightest ripples, or merest dimples mar the slab plane, frontpointing on microsmears is called for. Here, just the very front tip of the shoe is smeared, with the heel held relatively high. Contrary to popular belief, the best shoe for hard slab climbing is actually one with a stiffer sole, not a soft slipper-like one. A stiffer shoe will allow you to edge better, frontpoint, and smear better on miniscule holds without tiring your feet as much as a softer boot will.

For optimal performance of climbing sole rubber, temperature is key. This is especially true for

Peter Croft using proper edging technique on a steep slab—weight out and over the feet, heels slightly higher than the toes, heels in to the rock.

Peter Croft demonstrates the crossover step, frontpointing on edges.

hard friction climbs. Modern climbing rubber smears best at between 45°F and 55°F, so take on that slab test piece in the cool shade. Any dirt on your boot sole will be extremely detrimental, so meticulously clean your shoe soles before attempting that hard slab pitch. Rub off any dirt or grime, and clean the soles if necessary with a little water and a toothbrush. When properly cleaned, your soles should make a squeaking sound when you rub them hard with the palm of your hand.

Once shod, never walk around in the dirt. Dirt-impregnated soles are never the same. And never put chalk on your shoes—it greatly reduces your traction. Climbers discovered this fact in the '70s while working on a route called Hall of Mirrors on Glacier Point Apron in Yosemite. Many of the cruxes were as smooth as glass, and the first ascensionists discovered that any chalk dust on the footholds made it impossible for the feet to stick. By not using chalk, and subsequently not getting any chalk dust on the holds, they found that the smears worked.

Some of the most challenging slabs are difficult because they are sustained; meaning there are many difficult moves in a row without a big enough foothold to stop and rest. The key is to stay relaxed and focus on your breathing; steady, deep breaths will help you stay calm. When you get to a foothold where you feel comfortable, take advantage of it; shake out each leg, one at a time. On difficult routes I give myself a one-word mantra: "Relax." After each move I'll say it to myself: "Relax," mentally monitoring what muscles I'm firing the most and not tensing up more than I need to. After each move I'll think "relax"; do another move, "relax"; another move, "relax." Before I know it, I'm through the crux.

Today, with so many climbers learning technique in a vertical-walled gym environment, slab climbing has become somewhat of a lost art. But footwork is the foundation of all technique, and confidence in smearing establishes your connectivity to the rock, even on steeper routes.

Any aspiring trad climber can benefit greatly from a long apprenticeship on the slabs. The subtle tricks of balance and footwork, well learned from trial and error and time on the rock, can be applied later to steeper test pieces, where footwork still is the key to success.

In addition to mental poise and steady resolve, extreme slab climbing requires a quick mind to read the rock and decipher sequences, plus the exacting footwork and balance of a dancer. Successfully climbing what looks impossibly blank might be the sweetest victory of all.

Perhaps Royal Robbins summed it up best in his book *Basic Rockcraft*: "Slab climbing is a special art different from face climbing and crack climbing. Strength is less important, although strong fingers and sturdy foot muscles help. The expert slab climber is distinguished by grace and a cool mind. He keeps his weight over his feet and moves calmly and deliberately, as if he were only a foot off the ground. He does not rush. He looks ahead, carefully calculating his tactics, and acts with resolution. His footwork is neat and deft, for he realizes the importance of precise use of holds. And he concentrates totally on the problem in front of him."

Steep Face Climbing

In my work with the AMGA's Single Pitch Instructor Program, I've served as an examiner for their Single Pitch Instructor Assessment. It's a two-day exam where the candidates are tested on a variety of categories, including technical scenarios, client care, risk management, and teaching skills. On day two the candidates are presented with clients, and the goal is to accurately assess their abilities in a group setting in their role of instructor/guide.

Before this exam day I give candidates a list of potential topics and ask them to pick one for a lesson they'll present to the students. In one exam I had the opportunity to assess Wills Young, whose lesson was on face climbing technique. I've seen a lot of lessons on technique over the years, but Wills's stood out.

Wills was born in California but grew up in England, where he began face climbing on Gritstone. He moved back to California, living in Bishop for fourteen years, where he honed his face climbing skills on the granite of the Buttermilks boulders. He migrated to Chattanooga, Tennessee, where he runs an outdoor guiding/indoor coaching business along with Lisa Rands out of the High Point Climbing and Fitness gyms.

I've often said that you don't need to run 100 meters in 10 seconds to be a great track and field coach—but it helps, especially if you can effectively convey your knowledge verbally and with demonstration. Wills is one of those coaches. He's one of few humans to send a V14 boulder problem, and he is able to clearly and effectively communicate the fundamental mechanics of advanced techniques to his students.

When Wills gave his presentation on face climbing techniques, I took notes. I can honestly say that it was one of the best presentations on climbing techniques I've seen, and I've seen a lot of them. So when I began writing this book, I dug out the notes I'd scrawled down years ago.

Wills broke it down into these main principles:
1. Grip
2. Hip Position
3. The Push/Pull Principle
4. The Deadpoint Principle

Grip

THE CRIMP GRIP

The crimp is the key to exerting maximum power on thin edges and tiny holds.

It is by far your strongest grip, formed by placing your thumb alongside, and slightly over, your forefinger. Your finger pads should be directly on top of the hold, with the fingers flexed and bent at almost a 90-degree angle at the knuckle joint. On difficult face routes you'll generally be able to get only get two fingers on the holds, so by bringing the thumb into play you'll be making your grip 20 or 30 percent stronger, since you'll be using three fingers instead of just two.

OPEN-HANDED GRIP

For sloping holds, the open-handed grip allows you to get more of your finger and hand skin in contact with rock, thereby increasing friction. The key is

to stay below the hold to properly utilize it; you'll generate more friction when the elbow is down and against the wall and your weight is below it.

For training purposes, the open-handed grip is useful in that it puts less stress on the joints of the fingers, thereby reducing chances of developing finger joint problems and tendinitis.

The basic crimp grip

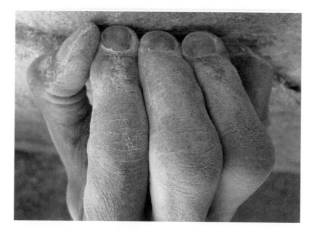
Crimping a large edge

The open-handed grip is most useful on big, rounded, and sloping holds.

Hip and back flexibility is an asset for overhanging face technique, allowing you to put more weight on your feet and less on your arms.

John Long using the open-handed grip on heinously sloping holds, Stoney Point, California, 1983

Hip Position

Hip position is the key to effective climbing technique for vertical and overhanging face climbing. Keeping your hips in to the wall takes weight off your arms—it's that simple. The goal is to put as much weight on the feet as possible throughout the climb. In most situations it's as easy as arching your back and consciously focusing on the position,

much like the cobra position in yoga.

Focus on your center of gravity and how it changes when you shift the position of your hips. When doing a high step, lead with your hips, shifting them in to the wall and in the direction you're stepping, until your center of gravity has shifted to that upper foothold. Being aware of your hip position is one of the easiest ways to improve your performance on overhanging face climbs.

HIP ROLL

If your hips are facing the wall, you're limited on how far you can reach up with one arm. For extended moves, you can gain a few inches by turning one hip into the wall. If you're reaching up with your left arm, turn your left hip in to the wall. You'll be able to reach several inches higher than if both hips are parallel to the wall. The opposite hand can be pulling straight down on a hold, or on a sidepull. If you're reaching up with your left hand,

Ron Fawcett, perhaps the best British climber of the 1980s, with a classic hip roll on Crank City (V4) at Joshua Tree, 1984

Erik Kramer-Webb performs a drop knee on Big Mo (5.11b) at Joshua Tree.

the left foot will naturally want to be positioned on the outside edge of the shoe.

DROP KNEE

If you have knee problems, you'll want to be careful with this technique. It allows you to position your hip very close to the wall, using footholds that otherwise would seem out of position. If you're reaching up with your right hand, you can use a high right foothold (using the outside edge of the boot); you swing your knee downward and roll your right hip in to the wall. Your left foot should be on the inside edge of the shoe. If you're utilizing a sidepull with your left hand, this technique will maximize your reach and keep your weight on your feet as you make the move.

Push/Pull Technique

The combination of pulling with your arms while at the same time pushing off with your legs is another key for success on difficult face climbs.

Good technique on an overhanging arête—arms straight, hips in to the rock, pushing with the left foot

1. John Long, dyno sequence at Stoney Point, 1983. First he plants his right foot and eyes the target hold.

2. In a single, powerful, fluid motion, he pulls with his arms and momentarily lets go with his left hand, latching the upper hold at the deadpoint.

If you draw an imaginary triangle from your two upper handholds down to a single point in the plumb line, that is the spot you'll want to plant one of your feet, especially if the wall is devoid of edges for your feet and you're utilizing a smear. Paste your foot in that line and push with your leg as you pull with both arms.

You can also use your arms in a push/pull combination, pressing down with the lower arm as you pull with the upper.

The Deadpoint Principle

Toss a ball up in the air. The moment the ball stops its upward progress and begins falling downward is the deadpoint.

3. After successfully latching the hold, it's time to reestablish footholds and carry on.

In rock climbing, you can use this principle of physics to your advantage for dynamic moves. With perfect timing, at the moment the deadpoint occurs, you'll feel a sense of temporary weightlessness, albeit for a microsecond.

The deadpoint principle works when you're reaching up with one hand or attempting to dyno with both hands. In both instances, lead with the hips; as you pull with your arm or arms, focus on coordinating the upward movement by thrusting the hips in, toward the rock.

If making a move with one hand, unweight your hand momentarily, timing it to coincide with the deadpoint, then, at that very moment, latch the top hold.

For full-on two-handed dynos, focus also on your footholds, bending the knees slightly and pushing off with both legs to give you more of an upward trajectory.

The best way to master the deadpoint principle is in the bouldering arena, practicing dynamic moves.

Mantles

For classic ledge mantles, look to see if the ledge slopes downward one way or the other. If the ledge is slightly lower to your right, it will be easier to get your right foot up on the ledge, which means the easiest mantle will be a left-hand mantle with your palm flat on the ledge, fingers pointing right. If the ledge is tiny, you can often make the mantle much easier by reaching up with the opposite hand (in this case the right hand) and finding an edge to crimp and pull down on.

If the ledge slopes downward to your left, it'll be easier to get your left foot up on the ledge, using a right-hand mantle, palm down on the ledge with your fingers pointing left.

If the ledge is wide enough and flat, it really doesn't matter what foot you step up with, and you can use both hands, about a foot apart, with palms pressed down and fingers pointing toward each other. Depending on the hold, sometimes it's best to flip the hand so that the wrist faces the wall and the fingers point outward.

OVERHANGING MANTLE

Overhanging mantles involve a more dynamic technique. Grab the mantle hold with both hands and set your feet as high as possible, focusing on precision with your footwork and keeping as much weight as possible on the feet. In one fluid motion,

1. On an overhanging mantle, be especially cognizant of your feet as you move up, placing the feet precisely on the holds.

2. As soon as you're high enough, in one quick motion, rotate your elbow up and flip your palm onto the mantleshelf.

pull hard with both arms; then, at the moment you're high enough, flip one elbow high enough so that the palm is pressing down. On difficult mantles with sloping and tiny holds, positioning the base

of the palm opposite the thumb utilizes the small bones at the base of the wrist. These bones are shaped roughly like a horseshoe and can be hooked on the best part of the hold.

3. Lock your arm and lean in so that your upper body's center of gravity is directly over your palm.

4. Then step up. Flexibility will pay off on difficult mantles.

TRAINING FOR MANTLES

If you do a lot of gym climbing, mantling technique may be one of your weaknesses, since unlike bouldering, you're rarely topping out on a flat ledge. Training for mantle strength is all about triceps strength. Two exercises to isolate the triceps and develop mantling strength are triceps extensions and dips. A solid triceps extension routine is three sets of eight repetitions several times a week. Adjust your weight so that you're barely able to complete the last rep. For dips, if you can easily do three sets of fifteen reps, hang some weight from your waist for extra resistance.

Crack Climbing Techniques

If you've done a lot of gym climbing but have never climbed outdoors, then crack climbing will seem unnatural, painful, and difficult for the rating. As a climbing school manager, I observe a typical profile for many of my students who signed up for guided climbing: extensive gym climbing, often up to 5.11, but when it came to crack climbing up real cracks on real rock, they often struggled mightily on 5.8.

Compared to face climbing, mastering crack climbing technique is a much tougher learning curve. Techniques are counterintuitive, and poor technique results in frustrating, painful failure. With the advent of a new generation of crack climbing gloves, painful hand wounds on the back of the hands (called "gobies") can be avoided, and I'd definitely recommend getting a pair when you're starting out.

Obviously, the difficulty of a particular crack is dependent on the size of your fingers and hands. If you have very small or very large hands, the difficulty rating of a particular climb might feel easier or more difficult than it's rated.

For crack climbing, a stiffer, more comfortable shoe will serve you better than a slip-lasted, gym-style shoe with an aggressive taper designed for overhanging face climbing.

You do not want to climb cracks with any rings on your fingers or bracelets on your wrist. Sadly, it's common for people to take a ring off and lose it in the field, so you might consider leaving rings at home for safekeeping.

Peter Croft, perhaps the best crack climber our sport has known, offers this advice for beginning crack climbers: "A classic mistake that newbies make is to toss a hand at a sharp jam and immediately tug on it. That would be wrong. Instead you want to take the time to feel inside the crack and experiment with a number of slight variations that still feel secure—milking it—until you find a jam that is at least relatively pain-free."

Finger Cracks

The thinnest jam-able cracks will accept your pinky finger, in the thumb-up hand profile, or the tip of your index finger, in the thumb-down position.

Look for places in the crack that form slight bottlenecks, where you can get the digit to jam, just like you would to place a nut. Only instead of jamming a metal chock, you're wedging your fingertip. In very thin and shallow cracks, you may only be able to get your finger in to the first knuckle.

On ultrathin cracks, look for places in the crack that are slightly offset, where one side sticks out a bit more than the other. This will allow you to use the edge of the crack like a sidepull or layback hold where no good jam exists.

Robert Finley solos Needle's Eye, Needles, South Dakota.

Thumb-up and thumb-down finger jams

Thumb-up finger jamming in an offset corner

As the crack gets a bit wider and deeper, you'll be able to do the classic "finger lock," when you can insert the index finger into the crack all the way to the third knuckle (which is where your finger meets the hand), thumb down. If you can get your index finger in past the second knuckle in a good constriction, this jam will feel very secure.

The thumb-down position feels more secure because as you move your elbow in toward your body as you move up, considerable torque is created at your fingers. For example, if you're jamming your right hand thumb down, as your elbow goes in toward your body, your pinky finger torques against

the right side of the crack as your index finger torques against the left wall of the crack.

Thumb Up or Thumb Down

One great advantage of jamming thumb up is that it allows you to reach much further for the next jam. Although a thumb-down finger lock will feel bomber, as you move up on the torqued fingers, you'll notice that when you get to about where your face is level with the jam, the torque on your wrist makes it very difficult to move your body higher. Using the same jam in a thumb-up position, you'll be able to easily pull on it to your chest or even waist level.

Going thumb up as much as possible in a vertical crack will allow you to reach further for each jam, thus climbing more quickly and efficiently, as you'll be doing fewer moves and fewer jams up the crack.

In an offset straight-in crack (where the left wall of the crack comes out toward you), the best approach would be to jam it left hand thumb up and right hand thumb down. This allows you to extend your fingers most ergonomically into the crack.

Of all the various types of jamming, climbing thin cracks feels most like face climbing, since your feet are typically on face holds adjacent to the crack or your feet are marginally torqued in the crack itself.

Taping the pinky finger and the index finger (since you'll be jamming either thumb up or thumb down) will allow the jams to feel much more comfortable—the tape provides a modicum of padding and prevents deep cuts if the edges of the constriction are very sharp.

The thumb stack, as seen from inside the crack

Off-hands (1 to 1¼ inch)

Between finger jams and thin hand jams is the dreaded "off-hand" size—too wide for the fingers to securely jam and too narrow for a thin hand jam.

While an off-width crack may seem more strenuous overall, this is perhaps the most technically difficult size to jam.

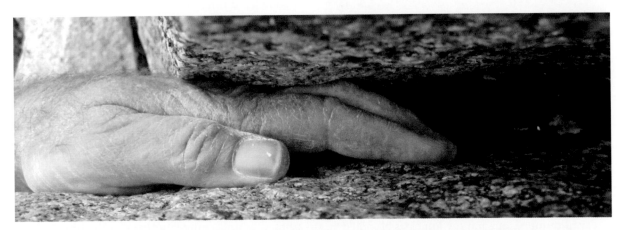

One way to jam an off-hand size crack is to insert the fingers as far as they can go, thumb up, then press with the fingers on one side of the crack, creating counterpressure against the back of the hand.

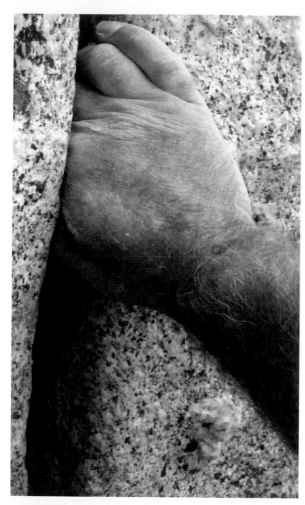

Off-hand jam, thumb down. Off-hand cracks re-quire combinations of thumb stacks and finger torquing.

In my college days (early 1980s), I spent my summers in Yosemite Valley. One summer I was lucky to have Werner Braun as a partner. Werner was one of Yosemite's top crack climbers, but he had a list of climbs he hadn't yet ticked off, mostly 11d crack climbs with the dreaded 1¼-inch jamming crux. I spent most of that summer getting my forearms pumped-out and my knuckles bloodied on those climbs. I can't say that I even came close to

mastering the technique, but I can say that I learned two basic strategies for off-hand jams following Werner up those climbs.

The first technique is known as "rattley fingers." This involves getting all four fingers in the crack, then twisting the fingers to gain a modicum of counterpressure against the walls of the crack. Since nothing really locks, this technique saps your hand and forearm strength rapidly if the crack has a sustained section of uniform off-hand width. Thumb down provides more torque and feels more secure than thumb up, but will not allow you to reach as far off the jam.

The second technique is to use the thumb cam or finger stack. This is accomplished by slipping your thumb into the crack, then curling the other fingers on top of it, wedging the thumb as you crank down on your fingers.

Hand Jams

To paraphrase the late Dean Potter, the famed Yosemite soloist who specialized in crack climbing:

"Dude, when my hand is jammed in a crack I AM ON BELAY."

I often joked that in an emergency, if Dean had a good hand jam, "you could tie off his wrist with a sling and use it for a rappel anchor."

Simply put, the hand jam is the most solid jam in all of crack climbing.

A thin hand jam is when you can barely get your hand into the crack all the way to the wrist. A slight flexion of the fingers (keeping the fingers straight and your thumb parallel to your index finger) produces some counterforce against both walls of the crack. Going with a thumb-down position creates torque to make the jam even more secure.

As the crack gets a bit wider, you can change the position of your thumb and move it across your palm, thus thickening your hand at the base of your palm. This is the classic hand jam.

Thin hand jam

The common misconception is that the hand jam works best by pressing the fingers against one wall of the crack, flexing the hand like a spring-loaded hinge to make it work.

To the contrary, the key to good hand jamming technique is to wedge the hand in the crack, done by bringing the thumb across the palm, which widens the base of the palm. This requires less hand and forearm strength than flexing the hand in the jam.

With hand jamming, the first thing to consider is whether you'll be jamming your hand thumb up

Hand jamming: Here the top hand is thumb down and the bottom hand thumb up.

The key to wider hand jams is to bring the thumb across the palm.

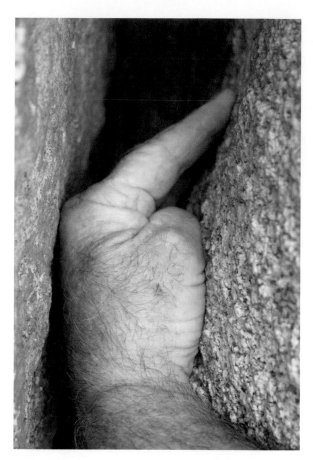

Wide hand jam: Note the placement of the thumb.

or thumb down. In general, thumb up is preferable, as it puts your hand in a more ergonomic position and allows you to make a longer reach to the next jam than if you were thumb down.

Once you insert your hand inside the crack, take a few seconds to feel where the crack jam will feel the least painful and most secure—called "milking the jam," then move your thumb down across your palm to create the wedging effect at the base of your palm. Then crank on it!

For a very wide hand jam or "cupped hand jam" the thumb can be placed against the index finger for added stability.

Footwork for Finger and Hand Cracks

One of the keys to good crack climbing technique is footwork—how to best jam your feet into the crack. Your legs are stronger than your arms, and getting the weight onto your feet and legs, and off your arms, is one of the most important aspects of good crack climbing technique.

In a straight-in crack, to jam the left foot, turn your knee to the outside (to the left) and present the narrowest profile of your shoe with your big toe up and the sole of your shoe parallel to the crack and perpendicular to the ground.

Foot jamming a "splitter" straight-in hand crack. The key concept is to turn the knee to the outside before inserting the foot, big toe facing up.

In ultrathin cracks, even if you can't get your toes in the crack, torquing the rand of your shoe against any offset or into any pocket in the crack can make a huge difference.

The most common mistake I see beginners make is not taking the time to accomplish this position and simply trying to punch their toe directly into the crack without turning the foot first.

Take the time first to turn your knee, then turn your foot, and place your toe in the crack. A spot where the crack narrows a bit to form a constriction will make for a better foot jam, as will a pocket in the crack.

With practice you'll find that you won't need to jam your foot as deeply into the crack as you might think (called over-jamming), because when you straighten out your leg and stand on your foot there will be quite a bit of torque at your ankle, camming your foot in place.

On very thin cracks and seams, the same basic technique applies, although you may only be able to get the edge of the sole of your shoe in the crack. In corners and seams where no crack exists, using the same basic mechanics and smearing the rand of your shoe (the rubber on the sides) will make a huge difference because of the torque you've created.

Fist Jams

Once the crack gets too wide for cupped hand jams, it's time to fist jam. You can jam your fist in a crack either palm in or palm out, depending on which configuration feels less awkward; either way you'll be wedging your fist into the crack like a chock, endwise (i.e., thumb on one side, pinky on the other).

You can change the size of your fist by changing the position of your thumb. For the smallest fist, take you thumb across your palm to the base of the pinky, then curl your other four fingers over the thumb.

Palm-down fist jam

Palm-up fist jam

To make your fist progressively larger, change the position of your thumb, placing the tip of your thumb between your fingers. Start with your thumb between your pinky and ring finger. To make it larger, place the thumb between the ring and middle finger, then between the middle finger and index finger; finally, for the largest fist jam, place the thumb outside the index finger, with the tip of your thumb against the index finger for stability.

The key to fist jamming, like all jamming, is to milk the jam before you commit to it. This means that with a relaxed grip, you feel the inside of the crack and determine where the fist will jam most securely, with the least amount of pain.

In narrow fist jams, start by turning your fist (either thumb up or thumb down, with your thumb parallel to the crack), insert your hand, then turn your hand until it starts to wedge.

Look for spots in the crack where there are subtle constrictions or pockets. Wedging your fist in a constriction (like placing a big hex) will be inherently more secure.

On diagonal cracks and cracks in corners, you'll generally want to fist-jam palm in with the top hand and palm out with the lower hand, shuffling the hands as you proceed.

Off-Width

This is the crack size wider than a fist jam but too narrow to get all of your body inside the crack. Of all the techniques in rock climbing, off-width crack climbing is without a doubt the most strenuous.

I can recall many times in Yosemite, at the top of a long sustained off-width crack, feeling like I'd puke from the exertion, utterly exhausted. A 5.10a off-width crack in Yosemite will feel more like a 5.12 level of exertion to the uninitiated.

Tony Sartin on Pratt's Crack (5.9), Pine Creek, California

In the early 1960s the first climbs in Yosemite Valley to be rated 5.10 were fearsome off-width climbs. The route names give insight into the difficulties involved: Crack of Doom, Crack of Despair, Twilight Zone.

The great free soloist Alex Honnold puts it this way: "Imagine doing wrestling with somebody with a cheese grater, and every time they get you into a lock they cheese grate you as hard as they can. You're like 'OUCH!!!! Off-width climbing sucks.'"

Peter Croft sums it up well: "While hand and finger cracks have most face climbers scratching their heads at first, off-width cracks add gut-wrenching nausea to the picture. This is because every part of your body comes into play. Going to failure in an off-width is like battling a giant anaconda—and losing."

Why are off-widths so strenuous? It's because no one part of your body can lock or jam securely or comfortably in the off-width crack size.

The first thing to consider is what side of your body you want to place in the crack. If the crack is in a corner and one wall comes out toward you, it's best to put your back against the wall that comes out toward you.

For example, if the crack is straight in, and the left wall of the crack comes out toward you, use

Erik Kramer-Webb displays a classic "chicken wing" on Hobbit Hole (5.10), Joshua Tree, California. Note the heel-toe jam.

Arm bar

your back on the left wall and place your left arm and left leg in the crack. This way you'll be able to use your right hand, thumb down, on the right edge of the crack.

Heel-toe jam

The basic technique is to insert one arm into the crack, using the arm bar or chicken wing technique, with the other hand pawing thumb down on the edge of the crack. In the narrowest of off-widths, you may be able to do a knee jam by placing your leg into the crack, then flexing your leg to make the knee/thigh bigger and getting it to wedge. Another important foot technique is the heel-toe jam, with your toe on one side of the crack and your heel on the other.

The length of the heel-toe jam can be varied by angling your foot in the crack until it spans whatever width you're dealing with. For narrower cracks, splay your feet out at a 45-degree angle, then rotate your toe inward until your foot spans the width of the crack. When you wedge your foot, you'll want to have your toes slightly lower than your heel for the best jam.

When moving up, it's best to try very small moves and try to develop a rhythm when you find that a particular technique is working. The toughest off-widths are smooth, overhanging, with no rests and no footholds/handholds to give you a break from the difficulty.

Heel-toe jams, probably the most important technique for climbing off-widths

Hand Stacks

Also called "Leavittation," hand stacking is named for the great Southern California climber Randy Leavitt, who developed this off-width technique. There are a variety of two-handed stacks that can be used: back of hand against back of hand, fist against palm of the hand, double fists, etc.

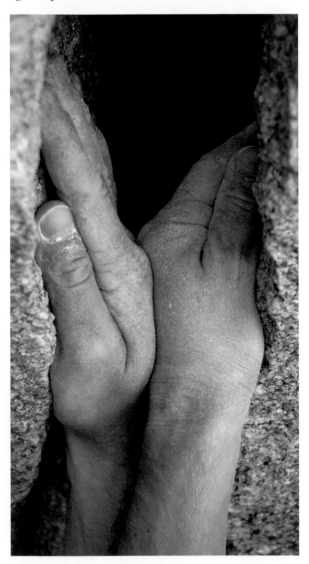

Hand stacking, also known as "Leavittation"

For hand stacks to work, to make upward progression, some part of the lower body must be wedged in order to move the hands higher. Usually the knee jam is used by placing the entire leg into the crack, then bending the leg at the knee to expand the muscles surrounding the knee, hopefully locking the knee in the crack.

Chimneys

Squeeze Chimney

The next size crack, just wider than off-width, is another physically demanding size, known as a squeeze chimney. Unlike the off-width, which is too narrow to get your whole body inside, you'll be able to get your entire body into a squeeze chimney. The only problem is, because the chimney is so narrow, it's tough to get good counterpressure against both walls of the chimney. The basic counterpressure strategy for the upper body is to push with both hands in front of you, exerting counterpressure between your arms and back while with the lower body exerting counterpressure between your knees in front of you and feet on the wall behind you.

If the crack is narrow enough, the use of the heel-toe jam can be a godsend, essentially allowing you to rest and/or move up off a solidly jammed foot. It takes practice to get good at squeeze chimneys, which can be extremely strenuous, but focus on this: If you're flailing and expending a lot of energy, slow down and concentrate on better technique, using less strength. Make small moves and focus on what's working, trying to develop a rhythmic pattern, and keep moving until a good rest spot is reached.

Like any new technique, it's best to start easy and work your way up the grades.

Back and Foot Chimneys

When the chimney gets a bit wider than a squeeze chimney, it's possible to use the knee-foot combo. This is when you place your knees on the wall in front of you then place the soles of your shoes on the wall behind you. With your upper body, you can press your palms against the wall in front of you, creating counterpressure between your back and arms. Moving one arm or leg at a time allows you to wriggle your way up the chimney in a series of small moves.

Erik Kramer-Webb demonstrates a heel-toe jam with his right foot and a knee-foot combo with his left leg on a flared chimney.

A bit wider is the classic chimney size that can actually be quite fun—a width where it's comfortable to span the chimney with your back on one side and your feet on the other. You can move with different combinations of counterpressure: back-hands, back-feet, opposite hands (one hand in front of you, pushing with your palm, the other hand behind you, pushing down with the palm), opposite feet, etc.

When the chimney gets even wider, you can use a full bridging/stemming position with your arms and legs, using the principle of counterpressure: opposite hand and foot. The widest chimney you can span, which I've done a few times, is using both hands on one side, and both feet on the other.

Flared Chimneys

A flared chimney is one in which the walls of the chimney are not parallel to each other, and not a uniform width apart. For example, in a drastically flared chimney, the walls of the chimney may present themselves at a 45-degree angle relative to each other.

My rule for flared chimneys is to face the flare. In other words, if you're facing the chimney and the right wall comes straight out at you, perpendicular to the plane of the rock face, and the left wall is slightly angled away from you, the left wall is the flared side you want to face. This allows your back to be flat against the right wall of the chimney while your feet can smear and utilize footholds on the flared left side. The exception to the rule would be if the non–flared side of the chimney has numerous obvious hand- and footholds. Then I'd face that way.

Liebacks and Underclings

A lieback is another counterpressure technique, used primarily to climb flakes and corners, where both hands pull on the edge of the crack as both feet push on the wall in opposition. If you think about it, in the lieback mode your legs and arms are working

Liebacking a thin crack. The higher you position your feet, the more stable your position, although the higher you put your feet, the harder you'll have to crank with your arms to maintain the counterpressure.

Carmen Cendejas underclings on Norm (5.10a), Joshua Tree, California.

against each other. The higher you move your feet, the more strength you'll need to use pulling with the arms. As your feet are placed lower, you'll need less force exerted by your arms, but it's a delicate balance—if your feet are too low, you'll lose the oppositional counterforces and your feet will slip.

Becoming confident and proficient at liebacking takes practice. The keys to focus on are relaxing your hand grip as much as possible, so as to not pump out your forearms, and keeping the feet relatively high—but not too high, as this will put unnecessary strain on the arms. Be keenly aware

of any footholds you can utilize on the face, as any foothold will take weight off the arms. If you're liebacking a crack in a corner, look for foot jams for your inside foot (foot closest to the corner); also look for stemming possibilities, bridging one foot on each side of the crack.

The undercling technique is similar to a lieback, different only in that you'll be grasping the edge of the crack or flake with both hands palm up. The most stable position will be when your feet are as high as possible, but this also requires the most strength from your arms. If the feet are too low, you'll lose the counterpressure and your feet will slip—so once again it's about finding the balance between keeping the feet too high and using more strength versus too low and not enough opposing pressure. Any foothold will make the undercling significantly easier, particularly on a steep face.

Stemming

Whenever you're climbing a corner (also called a dihedral), look for stemming and bridging possibilities using your hands and feet in counterpressure. The basic principle is simple: opposite hand and foot. If you're stemmed out in a corner, bridging with the feet and palming with the hands, in order to move one of your feet higher you'll need to lock an opposite foot and hand. For example, if you want to move your right foot higher, you'll need to lock your left foot and right palm in opposition.

Stemming position. To move her right foot higher, she'll need to lock her left foot and right palm in opposition. Remember the rule for counterpressure in corners: opposite hand and foot.

Crack Gloves

Years ago, crack gloves were cumbersome, felt clunky on the hand, and it seemed that only beginners would wear them. In recent years crack gloves have been redesigned with performance in mind, with a much thinner and user-friendly design, and even expert crack climbers have been seen using them. My favorite brands are Outdoor Research and Ocun.

In recent years, new and improved crack climbing gloves have appeared on the market. The new, more user-friendly designs have revolutionized crack climbing glove performance.

Taping Up

Crack climbing can be brutal on the hands, especially in a place like Joshua Tree. Taping up will help you milk the jams without ripping your skin. Tincture of benzoin (Cramer Tuf-Skin comes in a spray-on version) will help the tape job stick.

If you tape your hands too tightly, it will impede circulation and you'll get pumped faster. In this sequence, Joshua Tree guide Erik Kramer-Webb demonstrates one method of taping that allows good hand circulation.

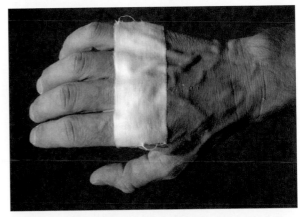

1. Start with a strip across the knuckles.

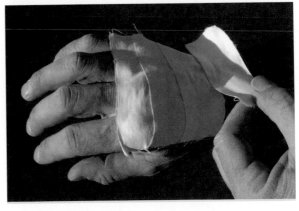

2. Continue laying tape down toward the wrist.

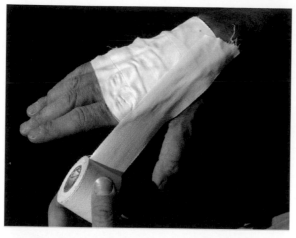

3. Lay a strip down between the thumb and forefinger.

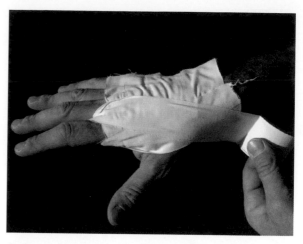

5. Smooth out the wrinkles.

4. Bring it back around between the thumb and forefinger.

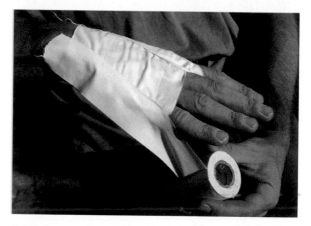

6. Make a strip between the pinky and ring finger.

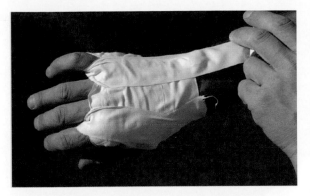

7. Bring the strip back down to the wrist.

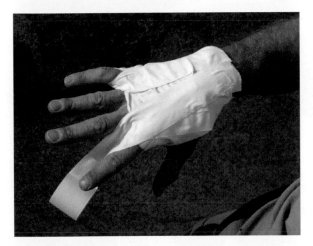

8. Make another strip between the index and middle fingers.

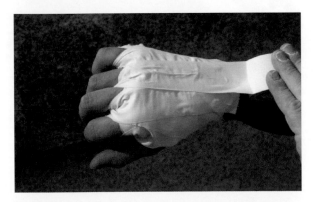

9. Make another strip between the middle and ring fingers.

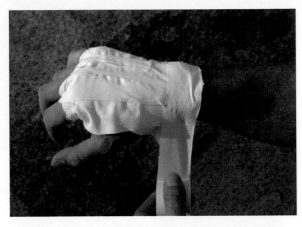

10. Wrap the tape around the wrist, but not so tightly as to compromise hand circulation and wrist flexion.

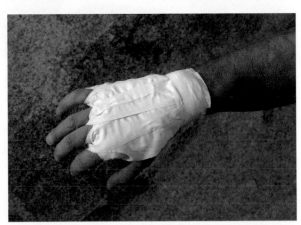

11. Good to go!

Anchoring

Rock Assessment

The first thing to think about when building anchor systems is the integrity and structure of the rock itself. Catastrophic anchor failures have occurred not because the gear placements were bad or the rigging was flawed, but because the rock itself was unsound. Determining good rock structure and knowing what to watch out for are fundamental requirements to build safe anchors.

When placing gear, the ideal crack is what guides call "a crack in the planet," a deep fissure that runs perpendicular (i.e., at a right angle) to the plane of the rock face, cleaving a massive, solid face of granite.

In general you'll want to avoid two things: detached blocks and flakes. A detached block is just that—a chunk of rock that is not attached to the main rock structure, but either is sitting on top of the cliff like a boulder or is part of the main rock face but completely fractured with cracks on all sides.

To assess a block, start by looking at its size. How big is it? Is it the size of your refrigerator, your car, or your house? Putting a piece of gear in the crack beneath a smaller block is a very bad idea. When the piece is weighted, it has a prying effect outward on the block. Even large blocks can shift easily, as I've encountered when boulder-hopping

Use good judgment if anchoring to detached blocks. Avoid small blocks and those resting on an inclined slab. I've adopted a rule from Yosemite Search and Rescue protocol: For a detached block to be used as a sole, monolithic anchor, it must be as big as a full-size refrigerator, situated lengthwise on a flat surface.

around car-size blocks, only to have one shift under my body weight. Look at how the block is situated. Is it perched down low, where it cannot slide out? Does it rest on a flat surface, or is it resting on an inclined slab? Generally, be very skeptical of using detached blocks as part of your anchor system, especially smaller blocks.

Flakes should also be avoided. A flake is formed by a crack in the rock that runs parallel to the main rock face. It can be wafer thin or several feet

This three-piece gear anchor looks great, except for one thing: bad macrostructure. Any force on the anchor could move the entire block, since it's cracked on all sides. Remember, the number-one cause of catastrophic anchor failure is bad macrostructure.

This camming device has been placed behind a flake of rock. If the cam is loaded, it will pry outward, potentially breaking the flake.

thick. A flake is inherently weak, since any gear placement, when loaded, will exert a prying effect outward on the structure of the flake, which can fracture if not strong enough to bear the force. In a naturally weak rock, like sandstone, a thin flake of rock can be extremely weak.

At Joshua Tree there is a climb named Exfoliation Confrontation that has a memorable crux where you reach underneath and undercling a flake of rock. Exfoliation is a natural process of granite formations and is the key in the formation of domes. Flakes of granite are layered, like layers of an onion, and the outer layer peels off from time to time due to the effects of weathering and gravity, exposing a new layer beneath.

One of the largest examples of exfoliation I've ever seen occurred in Yosemite Valley on a hot July day in 1996 at the Glacier Point Apron. An enormous flake, roughly the size of a football field and about 4 feet thick, detached from a point high on

This block is not as big as a fridge but is being incorporated into a larger anchor system. Its position is low and locked in by surrounding blocks, making it secure for this application.

analyzing rock structure, act like a geologist and scrutinize the rock and its various formations very carefully. To more finely test the soundness of the

the cliff, shearing off in one gigantic piece. After a 2,000-foot free fall, the impact resulted in a massive explosion, creating a 300-mile-per-hour shock wave of wind that felled 1,000 pine trees in a wide swath. A tourist, in line at the Happy Isles snack bar over 0.25 mile away, was killed when hit by a piece of the shrapnel from the blast.

When building anchors, look with skepticism at any flake. How thick is it, and how well attached to the main rock structure or cliff face? Test its soundness by thumping on it with the palm of your hand. Does it vibrate? Is there a hollow sound? When

I came across this "rappel anchor" at Tahquitz Rock in Southern California. You don't have to be a geologist to figure out that this flake is ready to exfoliate. Luckily, whoever rappelled off it survived the "exfoliation confrontation." Almost every catastrophic anchor failure is due to rock structure failure.

rock, take a carabiner and tap it against the rock. Differences in the sound you hear will reveal subtle differences in the rock structure.

Macro to Micro Rock Assessment

When assessing rock structure, evaluate from macro to micro. Macro is the big picture. Look at the main rock face. Is there a massive, solid rock structure? Is there a crack in the planet? Or are the cracks an intricate matrix where no real massive piece of completely solid rock exists. Are you dealing with blocks or flakes? Can you avoid using them? These are questions you need to ask. Never blindly place gear in cracks without first scrutinizing the big picture: the overall structure and integrity of the rock itself.

Microstructure is what's inside the crack you'll be using. Is the surface of the rock rotten, grainy, dirty, or flaky? Are there hollow spots or hollow flakes inside the crack itself? Microstructure can

This detached flake is a great example of bad rock structure.

Bad microstructure: The right side of this nut rests on a fragile flake.

The camming device placement looks great—nice and tight in a parallel-sided crack. But how good is the rock quality? Close inspection reveals a microstructure problem on the crack's left wall, rendering the placement less than ideal.

affect the integrity of your placements as much as the overall macrostructure.

Natural Anchors

Natural anchors utilize the natural features you'll find at the crag environment, such as trees, and the configuration of the rock itself. Trees are plentiful in some areas, rare in others, like in a desert environment. When assessing the reliability of a tree, there are several considerations. Is the tree alive or dead? What is the environment (dry or wet)? What is the diameter of the tree's trunk? How deeply rooted is the tree? Is it rooted in soil, sand, or gravel?

How strong are trees? In 2015 John Morton, a search and rescue technician with Snohomish County Search and Rescue and Everett Mountain Rescue in Washington state, published an extensive study of the strength of trees in the Pacific Northwest. What he found was interesting. Trees that grew in areas with routinely high winds were stronger than trees not subjected to high winds. His findings: in an area that reached wind speeds of 65 miles per hour, no tree trunk over 28-inch circumference (9-inch diameter) tested less than 25 kN (5,620 lb.) breaking strength. This included pine, cedar, maple, cottonwood, alder, and hemlock trees. In areas with less wind, trees are weaker.

Based on Morton's study, I'd recommended these assessment criteria for a tree to be used as a sole, monolithic natural anchor:
1. Living and structurally dense (not hollow)
2. Trunk is vertically aligned
3. Deeply rooted in soil (not growing out of cracks in the rock)
4. Symmetrically round trunk at ground level
5. Minimum diameter of 12 inches

When setting up a toprope anchor, use two separate trees in the anchor system if possible. If only one tree is available, and it's smaller than 12 inches in diameter, back it up with another gear placement or two.

The rock itself can be used for anchoring. Look for large spikes or horns of rock attached to the main rock structure to tie off as part of your anchor. A tunnel in a solid rock structure is called a thread, and it is utilized by threading a sling or cord, or tying a rope, through the tunnel. Limestone is a rock type with many threads, whereas threads are a rarity in granite.

Use detached blocks with caution. They should be well situated, unmovable, and not top-heavy. I've adopted a guideline from Yosemite Search and Rescue protocol: For a granite block to be used as a

OK. A properly girth-hitched nylon sling.

Good. A double-length (48-inch) nylon sling tied with an over-hand knot makes the sling itself redundant.

Good. A figure eight follow-through knot used to tie the anchor rope directly to the tree.

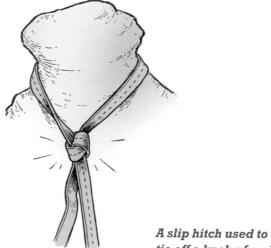

A slip hitch used to tie off a knob of rock.

touch each other. This way, even if the block shifts slightly, I still am anchored to the mass of the block.

When tying off blocks, watch for sharp edges that may fray or cut your rigging rope, and use padding or an edge protector when needed.

A friend of mine put up a new route at Joshua Tree—a 40-foot-high sport climb with five bolts—up the face of a massive block that was a

Although you can't see it in the photograph, this solid rock bollard is connected at its base to the main rock structure, what I call "attached to the planet" rather than a block "sitting on top of the planet." Since the doubled cordelette is tied with a figure eight on a bight, and the rope is clipped to two opposed and reversed carabiners, the rigging itself is redundant.

How to tie a slip hitch. The slip hitch can be tightened by pulling on one strand, making it more secure than a girth-hitch for tying off knobs of rock.

sole, monolithic anchor it must be as large as a full-size refrigerator lying lengthwise on a flat surface. Avoid using blocks resting on a slanting surface or a slab. I like to tie off the block around its entire mass, rather than using the pinch where the block touches another rock surface or where two blocks

A "thread" is a sling or cord threaded through a tunnel in the rock, rare in granite but common in limestone. Here the cordelette is doubled, threaded through the tunnel, then tied off with an overhand knot, creating a very strong four-loop master point. But what about the structural integrity of this mini rock-arch, which appears to be slightly cracked? This thread is in granite, reliable if the pull is straight down on the thicker section of the rock. In sandstone, which is a weaker rock, I'd consider this anchor to be unreliable.

facet of a larger cliff. One day I got a phone call: "Tony's route fell down!" I didn't believe it until I walked out there and saw it with my own eyes. The gigantic block was top-heavy and had simply toppled over, with the side where Tony's route was now straight down in the dirt, leaving behind a void in the cliff the size of a small house. I got down on my hands and knees and peered underneath. I could see one of the bolt hangers! Bouldering legend Chris Sharma visited the site shortly thereafter, climbing what is now one of Joshua Tree's most difficult boulder problems, up the newly exposed overhanging face of one side of the block.

A single, bombproof natural anchor (that I refer to as a "monolith") can safely be used for a rappel or toprope anchor—like a 3-foot-diameter

A monolithic tree anchor. This massive live pine tree is 60 feet tall and well rooted at its base. Both the cord and the carabiners are doubled for redundancy in the rigging.

This beefy horn of rock is "attached to the planet," part of a massive structure of rock, which is what you're looking for, rather than a detached block sitting "on top of the planet." The cordelette is doubled around the horn and tied with an overhand knot, making the cord itself redundant—an extra precaution to safeguard against the cord being cut by an edge.

ponderosa pine tree, or a knob of rock the size of your refrigerator that's part of the main rock structure. Just make sure that your sling or rope around the anchor is redundant. For example, when rigging a rappel anchor around a massive tree, use two separate slings with two rappel rings to gain redundancy in your anchor system, at least in the rigging. When rigging a belay or toprope anchor, loop two strands of the cordelette around the tree, then tie a figure eight knot for a two-loop master point. Clip in with two carabiners, opposed and reversed, and you have redundancy in your anchor rigging (although

technically, one single tree is nonredundant). Always use caution and sound judgment when using a single, monolithic natural anchor.

Nuts

The Evolution of Chockcraft

A chockstone is simply a rock wedged in a crack. Naturally occurring chockstones can be as small as a pebble or as big as a house. The notion of using a chockstone for an anchor dates back to the origins of the sport. In the late 1800s in the British Isles, rock climbers began using natural chockstones for anchors by slinging a cord around them and attaching their rope to the sling with a carabiner. The use of artificial chockstones—called chocks, or, more commonly, nuts—began in the early 1960s, at a cliff in North Wales of all places, at a crag named Clogwyn Du'r Arddu. The hike up to the crag followed a railroad track, and some ambling climber picked up a nut along the way and pocketed it. Up on the cliff he threaded a small cord through the nut before wedging it in a constriction in a thin crack. Thus the subtle art of chockcraft was born.

In American rock climbing, until the 1970s pitons were used almost exclusively for protection and anchors. In Europe pitons were made of soft iron, and once hammered into a crack they were nearly impossible to remove and reuse. Legendary American climber John Salathe, a wrought-iron worker by trade, developed the first hard steel pitons, forged from an old Ford Model A axle, which he used for his famous ascents in Yosemite Valley during the 1940s. These high carbon steel pitons could be driven and then removed, over and over again.

Yvon Chouinard refined and innovated the design of chrome moly steel pitons from 1957

A selection of chocks from the 1970s. Nuts have evolved over the years but are still based on the same original basic designs.

to 1965, improving on Salathe's designs with the introduction of knifeblade, horizontal (called the Lost Arrow), and angle pitons. These pitons revolutionized big wall climbing in Yosemite during the "Golden Age" of the 1960s, where hundreds of placements were required for the ultimate big wall climbs in Yosemite, like El Capitan. Once placed, they could be removed by the second, leaving the climbing route in the same condition for the next climbing team. Climbing standards in Yosemite led the world at the time.

But it came with a price. On popular climbs in Yosemite, the repeated pounding and removal of hard steel pitons began to permanently damage the cracks, leaving ugly "pin scars" every few feet up crack systems. Cracks were getting "beat out," and something had to be done. In Yosemite the National Park Service actually closed down a few climbs because of piton damage.

When the great American climber Royal Robbins made a trip to England in the 1960s, he saw how effective nuts could be, and he imported the idea back to Yosemite. His 1967 ascent of The Nutcracker, one of Yosemite's most popular climbs, was done entirely with nuts, Royal's way of showing that nuts were a viable alternative to the destructive pitons. Climbing the route today, you'll notice there still are piton scars on the route, a testament to how slow American climbers were to embrace the new and more gentle technology of chockcraft—a big change from bashing hard steel pitons into cracks with heavy blows from a hammer.

The change was finally precipitated by the fact that many cracks were simply being destroyed. Even granite is relatively soft when compared to cold hard steel. But it wasn't until Yvon Chouinard introduced chocks to American rock climbers in his 1972 equipment catalog, and Doug Robinson espoused the virtues of nuts in his seminal treatise *The Whole Natural Art of Protection*, that the American climbing community firmly embraced the idea of "clean climbing," a new ethic where climbing anchors were placed and removed without scarring or damaging the rock.

Today there are thin crack climbs in Yosemite where for hundreds of feet every finger jam is in an ancient piton scar, although now instead of using pitons, nuts can be slotted into the V-shaped bottom of the old pin scars.

Artificial chocks now come in a dazzling array of shapes and sizes, the largest ones capable of holding more than 3,000 pounds and the tiniest micronuts designed to hold body weight only. The hexentric, commonly called a hex, is a unique six-sided nut with four distinct attitudes of placement, first introduced by Chouinard Equipment in 1971. It was followed by the Stopper in 1972, with its simple but effective tapered trapezoidal shape. Although there have been many new designs introduced since then, they are basically variations on a theme to these classic and timeless designs, which are still as viable today as they were almost fifty years ago.

Another ingenious design, called the Tricam, invented by Jeff Lowe in 1980, is essentially a single cam that can be used either passively or actively. Since it has a tapered design, with a point on one end, it can be wedged like a nut (called a passive placement) or used like a cam (called an active

A selection of modern-day nuts

placement), where a mechanical action (i.e., camming) takes place. The camming action occurs when the sling is loaded on the back, or spine, of the cam, between two rails that contact the rock on one side of the crack, creating a force that pivots like a fulcrum onto the pointed end on the other side of the crack. The design is useful for many horizontal crack situations, but it can be somewhat difficult to remove with one hand or once it is weighted.

When placing a nut, or any other piece of gear for that matter, again, the first thing to consider is the overall integrity of the rock itself. I can't over-emphasize the importance of rock assessment. Nuts have very low holding power in soft sandstone, or rotten or flaky rock. Avoid placing nuts in cracks under or around detached blocks, or in cracks behind loose flakes. Look for "straight-in" cracks in

The classic designs of the hex (top) and the Stopper (bottom) have changed little since their inception in the early 1970s.

Piton scars on a Yosemite crack

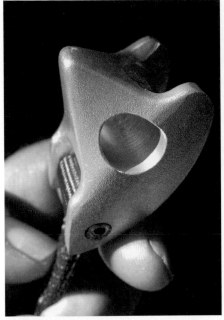

The Lowe Tricam

Tricam in camming mode

Tricam in passive mode

massive rock structure, where the crack runs perpendicular to the plane of the rock face.

Once a good crack system is found, look for obvious constrictions in the crack itself. A "bottleneck" placement is found where the crack tapers drastically, and the proper size nut is fitted in the narrowing constriction.

With a basic tapered nut, like the Stopper, the preferred placement is in the narrow configuration, since this setting has the most surface contact and stability. The wider endwise configuration is an option for narrow slots and shallow cracks, but it ultimately has less surface contact and generally less stability.

The typical nut placement is in a vertical crack, but horizontal cracks will work if there is a narrowing at the lip of the crack and you can slide a nut in from the side, then pull it into the constriction.

The real art of chockcraft comes into play with the more subtle placements. Look for any slight variations in the walls of the crack. When placing a

Stopper in a bottleneck placement. There is simply no way that in a downward pull the nut could be pulled through the bottleneck—something would have to give, either the rock itself or the nut or wire cable breaking. Grade: B+.

Very good. This Stopper placement is in good, solid rock and has flush surface contact on both sides of the nut. I'd grade this one an A-.

This endwise Stopper placement has good surface contact on both sides, although the crack is slightly flared. Grade: B-.

Bad. The left side of this nut lacks surface contact with the rock. Grade: D-.

nut, aim for maximum surface contact between the metal faces of the chock and the walls of the crack.

When the walls of the crack are virtually parallel sided, using the camming action of a Tricam or hex is the best option for a nut placement, although this is territory that spring-loaded camming devices were designed for. When you're starting out and new to placing nuts, unless you can see an obvious, V-shaped taper in the crack, chances are you won't be able to get a reliable nut placement.

Of paramount concern when placing a nut is the direction of pull. In what direction will the chock be loaded? Most placements can withstand a pull in only *one* direction. While the nut may be able to withstand a load of 2,000 pounds in that one direction, the slightest tug in the opposite direction might jerk the nut right out of its

placement. When incorporating a nut placement into an overall anchor system, look at the ultimate direction in which your anchor system will be loaded, and equalize your placement in a line toward this focal point (called the master point).

Setting a nut properly is also important. Many novice climbers make a great nut placement but fail to set it properly, which makes the nut susceptible to levering out of its placement if pulled from a different angle than intended. Setting the piece is accomplished by simply applying several stout tugs in the direction the piece will be loaded, most easily accomplished by attaching a sling to the nut with a carabiner and yanking on the sling, firmly wedging the nut in its intended placement. While this definitely makes the nut more difficult to remove, it is an important concept that many novices miss.

OK. This Stopper is in a good bottleneck but is not set deeply enough inside the crack. Since it lacks surface contact on its left side, it is susceptible to failure in any outward pull. Grade: C.

Good. The left side of this nut is nearly 100 percent flush, and the curve of the nut on its right side fits the curve of the crack. Grade: A.

Good. This nut has excellent surface contact on both sides, plus the lip on the right side of the crack protects against any outward force. Grade: A.

Fail. Poor surface contact, on both sides; there's insufficient narrowing of the crack below the placement. Might hold body weight, but might not. Grade: F.

Excellent. This hex placement has near perfect flushness on both faces of the nut in a solid, straight-in crack. Loading the nut's cable will kick in the camming action of the hex. Grade: A+.

Good. This hex is in a narrowing pocket, and both sides of the nut have good surface contact. Grade: A-.

Bad. No surface contact on the left side makes this hex placement likely to fail with the slightest outward force. Grade: D-.

Bomber. This perfectly flush endwise placement couldn't be any better. Grade: A+.

Relatively flush on both sides, but the rock micro-structure is grainy, with large crystals, and the right wall of the crack flares out a bit. Grade: C+.

A nice, flush fit. Hard to grade this one, since the placement is only as strong as the rock structure itself, and I'm concerned about the possibility of the rock itself fracturing. Grade: B-.

A nut tool is indispensable for removing chocks. Here are two models: Black Diamond (top) and Metolius (bottom).

To remove a nut with a nut tool, inspect the placement and determine its intended direction of pull, then tap in the opposite direction.

Carrying a nut tool, a metal pick designed for nut removal, facilitates "cleaning" nuts. Cleaning a nut can be as easy as yanking it in the opposite direction from the intended direction of pull, but be careful with recalcitrant nuts that can suddenly pop out and hit you in the face or teeth. Yanking a piece out can also send your hand bashing into the rock, scraping your knuckles. A better approach to removing a nut is to use the nut tool, giving the nut a tap opposite from the direction of loading. For larger nuts, an easy way to loosen them is to tap the nut with a carabiner, metal to metal.

Becoming skilled at chockcraft takes practice. Buy a selection of nuts and find a crag with plentiful crack systems at the base of the cliff. Practice rock assessment. Look for good rock structure, preferably a straight-in crack. Then look for any obvious V-shaped constrictions in the crack. If there is nothing obvious, look for any subtle narrowing of the width of the crack. Practice nut placements, aiming for maximum surface contact between

metal and rock, keeping in mind the paramount importance of direction of pull. Set the nut with a sharp tug. Once set, it should not move, pivot, or wiggle in its placement when you test it with a slight tug in the opposite direction of the intended direction of loading. Practice will help you develop the knack for seeing what size nut you need for a particular placement, then selecting the proper nut and fitting it into the crack on the first try. To gain confidence quickly, take an anchoring class from a rock climbing school or hire a guide for a day of anchoring practice so you can be critiqued on your placements by a professional.

Every nut placement is different—some less than perfect, some bomber, some worthless. You should have enough knowledge to know what's good and what's not, and what constitutes a placement you can trust.

Cams

In the mid-1970s a stout, muscular fellow by the name of Ray Jardine could often be seen peering through binoculars, gazing upward at the various nooks and crannies on the walls of Yosemite Valley. With his thick beard and glasses he looked like a bird-watcher, but Ray wasn't looking for birds. The bulging forearms gave it away—Ray was a climber, and he was looking for the ultimate crack: one of those perfectly straight cracks that split Yosemite's steep walls like a surgeon's incision, shooting upward for 100 feet, uninterrupted.

Ray had invented a new technology—the spring-loaded camming device, or SLCD—that allowed him to place reliable protection in even perfectly parallel-sided cracks. When he found his ultimate crack climb, he swore his partners to secrecy and set out on a mission: to climb the most difficult crack ever climbed in Yosemite. He named it The Phoenix—a fingertip- to hand-size crack on a gently overhanging wall high above Cascade Falls in the lower valley. After dozens of attempts using his newfangled technology, he finally succeeded in climbing Yosemite's first 5.13. Ray called his miracle invention the "Friend," and soon the word was out. Some climbers called it "cheating"; others claimed it was "the greatest invention since the nylon rope."

Marketed by Wild Country, the Friend soon became an integral part of every rock climber's rack. Ray soon retired from climbing and, financed by his proceeds from the licensing of the Friend, went on to sail around the world, hike the Pacific Crest Trail, row across the Atlantic, and ski to the South Pole.

The idea of the SLCD, or "camming device" for short, is simple in concept yet complex in design. Jardine's original design consisted of a unit with a rigid aluminum shaft connected by an axle to four independent aluminum spring-loaded cams (called "lobes"). The cams retracted via a trigger bar that slid up and down a slot in the shaft. The unit was fitted into a parallel-sided crack with the cams retracted; when weight was applied to a sling tied into a hole in the bottom of the shaft, the cams were activated in response to the load. To keep the unit from being pulled out of the crack, a corresponding force held it in place. The downward force in the direction of the shaft was transferred outward at the cams, which generated an outward force against the walls of the crack.

The disadvantage of Ray's design was that a rigid shaft could not flex or bend in the direction of pull, an especially troubling problem for placements in horizontal cracks.

Today there is a huge array of SLCDs on the market, and the majority of these designs have flexible wire cable shafts instead of rigid ones. One of

The original Wild Country Friend was one of the greatest innovations in rock climbing.

Spring-loaded camming devices have become an integral part of every climber's rack.

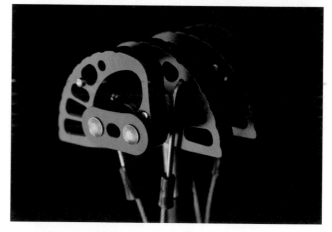

The Black Diamond Camalot was the first double-axle design.

The Metolius Power Cam has color-coded dots that help you assess your placement.

The Metolius offset TCU (three-cam unit) works well in slightly flaring cracks.

the biggest improvements since the invention of the Friend was the first double-axle design, called the Camalot, introduced by Black Diamond Equipment, which allows for a much greater range of placement of the cams. Now, in addition to units with four cam lobes, there are TCUs (three-cam units) and offset cams (for flared cracks).

Placing an SLCD

When placing an SLCD, the first thing to consider is rock quality. SLCDs can fail if the rock is soft, brittle, or loose. They can easily pull out if placed behind a small, loose block or thin flake of rock. In solid granite, in an ideal placement, a Black Diamond Camalot can hold as much as 14 kN (3,147 lb.). Never rely on a camming device to hold in very soft sandstone, or in rotten or flaky rock. Cam manufacturer Metolius advises: "Rock fails in two basic ways: Either a relatively large piece breaks off or the surface layer is crushed under the pressure of the cam lobe, allowing the cam to 'track out.' You must assess the integrity of the rock and choose the soundest possible location for your placements. Look for fractures in and around the walls of a

potential placement that could denote weakness, as well as pebbles, crystals, or micro-flakes that could snap off. Be extremely suspicious of placements behind flakes or blocks."

Since they rely on friction to a certain extent, camming devices are not as strong in exceptionally slick or polished rock, or rock that is wet or icy. Again, avoid placements behind detached blocks and loose flakes—the outward expansion of the cams can generate a tremendous force that can pry the rock loose. Look for straight-in cracks in solid rock. A straight-in crack is one that runs

The placement looks good, but how strong is that flake forming the left side of the crack? I wouldn't want to test it! Grade: F.

The inside cam lobes on this Black Diamond Camalot are open beyond the acceptable range, and the widening crack above the cams will allow the cams to easily "walk" into the wider section, even with minimal loading and unloading of the device, rendering the placement unstable and susceptible to failure. Grade: D-.

Very good placement. All the cams have good surface contact in a solid, straight-in crack, and the cams are in the recommended range for a Camalot (50 to 90 percent retraction). Grade: A.

perpendicular to the face of the rock, bisecting the rock at a right angle.

When placing a camming device, look for a section of the crack where the walls are uniformly parallel, or where they form a subtle pocket. Avoid widening cracks, where the crack is wider above the cams, as the camming device, due to its spring-loaded design, will naturally have a tendency to wiggle upward as the cam is activated. This phenomenon is known as "walking." This walking movement is most exaggerated when the piece is repeatedly weighted and unweighted, as in toproping. In a crack where the walls are uniformly parallel, or where the crack narrows slightly above the cams, if there is any walking, the cams will not open any wider and will stay within acceptable retraction range. As a test, grab the sling and yank and pull on it to see what walking, if any, occurs. This is an exaggerated test;

Bad. The two cam lobes on the right side of the crack are outside the acceptable range for a Camalot (too wide), and each set of cam lobes (inside and outside) are not symmetrically retracted. Grade: F.

Metolius cams have color-coded "range finder" dots on the edge of the cams to assist in assessing your placement. Green is the recommended range (75 to 100 percent retracted). Yellow means caution; you're slightly out of the optimal range—the next larger size cam will likely be a good fit. Red means danger; you're making a potentially bad placement. This placement's grade: A.

Good. This Metolius Power Cam displays optimal green "range finder" dots in a solid, parallel-sided crack. Grade: A.

when you actually use the piece, the force will be more constant. Any piece will "walk" if you yank back and forth on it with enough vigor. The key point is that this is something to be aware of and to watch for.

Poor. Although the range of retraction is acceptable, this Metolius Power Cam could easily walk up into the wider pod in the crack above the cams, rendering the placement unstable. Also, the outside right cam has poor surface contact and is too close to the edge of the crack. Grade: D.

Good. This Camalot is about 70 percent retracted, and all four cam lobes have good surface contact against the walls of a parallel-sided crack. Grade: A.

Metolius recommends that in a horizontal crack, the outside cams should be placed on the bottom of the crack for maximum stability like in this Camalot placement. Grade: A.

OK. A larger size cam would be better, but this Metolius Power Cam is in a pocket in the crack that lends some stability to the placement, even though it is borderline on the red "range finder" dots, signifying a marginal placement. Grade: C.

Too tight. Over-cammed, this Camalot is more than 90 percent retracted and will be difficult to remove. Grade: C-.

Right: Not ideal. Although Camalots will work in slightly flaring cracks, a parallel-sided crack is what you're looking for. Here, even though the crack is flared and the inside cams are retracted tighter than the outside ones, all four cams have good surface contact and are in the acceptable range of retraction. Grade: C+.

Bad. The crack is way too flared for this Metolius Power Cam, and the cam on the right side has very poor surface contact with the rock. Grade: F.

This Camalot fits nicely into this pocket in the crack. Grade: A-.

Another key to a good placement is the range of retraction on the cams. Black Diamond recommends that the Camalot be placed in the lower- to mid-expansion range (50 to 90 percent retraction), while Wild Country advises the following for its single-axle designs: "It is vitally important that all the cams make contact with the sides of the rock, preferably in the middle half of their expansion range (i.e., the cams should be one-quarter to three-quarters open)." Metolius recommends to "select the largest size cam that will fit without getting stuck. Cams should not be placed near the wide end of their expansion range. When a unit is loaded, it expands as the slack is removed from the system and the cams and rock compress. A nearly tipped-out cam won't have enough expansion left to accommodate this process. A loose cam is also more prone to walking and has little range left to adjust."

To illustrate what constitutes an acceptable range of retraction for the cams of a camming device, let's look at the Black Diamond Camalot in greater detail.

What is 50 to 90 percent retracted for a double-axle camming device like the Camalot? When you're looking at the Camalot without pulling on the trigger, it's at 0 percent retraction. Squeezing the trigger mechanism so that the cams are as tight as possible is 100 percent retracted. At 100 percent retracted, in a very tight placement, the Camalot will likely be very difficult to remove, and you

Good. This Metolius cam is in the tighter aspect of its range. Green means good to go. Grade: A.

While the placement looks good, the rock structure is questionable. How strong is that chunk of rock forming the right wall of the crack? Maybe OK in solid granite like this, but in a weaker rock like sandstone, when the cam is loaded the rock might fracture. Remember, the most important thing to consider when placing cams is the structural integrity of the rock. Grade: D-.

risk losing an expensive piece of gear. In the last 10 percent of the tightest aspect of the range (90 to 100 percent retracted), the Camalot also loses some of its holding power, another reason not to go too tight on a placement. The starting point for a good placement is at 50 percent retraction, which is when you pull the cams at least halfway tight. Looking at the base of the cams, 50 percent retraction is when the base of each cam is at a 45-degree angle relative to the vertical axis of the Camalot. If the cams are symmetrically retracted, they will be at a 90-degree angle relative to each other. A common mistake novices make is to place a Camalot near the outer limit of its range (0 to 50 percent

retraction). This can prove to be a very unstable placement if the unit moves at all in the crack, which can easily happen if the Camalot is placed in a crack that widens above the cams and the piece is repeatedly weighted and unweighted. Again, the optimal Camalot placement is when the cams are at least halfway tight (50 percent retracted). From the beginning position, pull the trigger mechanism until the range on the cams is half the starting size, then go only smaller and tighter from there. Scrutinize your placement after the camming device has been placed in a crack to make sure the cams are in the acceptable range.

Metolius cams have a unique color coding that assists you in assessment. The company gives this advice: "Verify that you have chosen the best size by making sure that the green Range Finder dots are lined up where the cam lobes touch the walls of the placement. Yellow dot alignment is okay too,

The same crack with two different placements. In the left-hand photo, notice how the left outside cam is very close to the edge of the crack. By flipping the cam around (right photo) the outside cam is now on the right wall, and the inside cam, now on the left wall, is deeper in the crack. Since the inside and outside cams are offset, flipping the cam one way or the other can often afford a better placement, particularly in shallow cracks in corners.

but you must exercise more caution with the placement, because the cam will be less stable, hence more prone to walking, and it will have less expansion range left to accommodate walking to a wider position. If the cam you choose aligns in the yellow zone, the next larger size will align perfectly in the green zone. Use that cam instead, if it's still on your rack. Never use a placement in the red zone unless it's the only placement available."

Study the literature that comes with any camming device you purchase and learn what the manufacturer recommends for the acceptable range of retraction and the various placement criteria. Most manufacturers also have informative PDF files on camming device guidelines that you can download from the company's website.

Becoming proficient in the use of camming devices takes thought and practice. To develop confidence quickly, hire a professional guide to critique your placements. Metolius suggests that you "practice placing cams in a safe venue, at ground level, before you trust your life to a cam placement.

This rack has a good assortment of both nuts and camming devices.

This process can teach you a lot, but written guidelines and practice are no substitute for qualified instruction. We strongly recommend that you learn to place cams under the supervision of a certified guide."

When I teach camming device placements, I first demonstrate the fundamentals then let the student make a variety of placements with a critique on each one. Working with a guide will allow you to learn from your mistakes before venturing out on your own. Better to learn in a "ground-school" setting than on your first toprope anchor that your "Friend" was no friend at all.

Toproping Rack

For toproping, you don't need the tiniest nuts and camming devices designed for aid climbing or body-weight placements; you'll want gear with an individual minimum breaking strength of at least 6 kN (1,349 lb.).

Buying more large nuts (like hexes) will save you money if you're on a budget, but camming devices will prove more versatile. Many experienced climbers rarely carry a full range of hexes these days.

Here is an example of a rack that will allow you to rig a toprope anchor system in most situations:

- 1 set of wired nuts from 0.5 to 2 inches (e.g., Black Diamond Stoppers, sizes 4–12)

- 1 set of hexes or tricams from 1 to 2.5 inches (e.g., Black Diamond Hexes, sizes 5–8, Camp (Lowe) Tricams, sizes 2–4)
- 1 nut tool
- 1 set of camming devices from 0.4 to 4 inches (e.g., Black Diamond Camalots 0.4, 0.75, 1, 2, 3), plus doubles on 1 and 2
- 6 single-length (24-inch) slings
- 2 double-length (48-inch) slings
- 2 cordelettes (18 to 20 feet of 7mm nylon cord)
- 1 length of low-stretch rope for rigging (10mm × 80 to 100 feet)
- 10 to 12 carabiners
- 4 to 6 locking carabiners

Fixed Anchors

Pitons

A piton is a metal spike that is hammered into a crack for an anchor. The blade of the piton is the part hammered into the crack, leaving the pro-truding eye into which you can clip a carabiner. Piton anchors are something of a rarity these days, but occasionally you'll come across fixed pitons (also called pins) at the top of a crag. Follow these steps before using any fixed pin. First, assess the rock structure and look at the crack where the piton resides. Is it behind a block or flake, or is it in a straight-in crack with good structure? A good piton should be driven in all the way to the eye, and should not wiggle when you clip into it with a sling and pull on it to test it. The piton itself should not be excessively corroded or cracked. (Look closely at the eye of the piton, as this is usually where the piton will be cracked.) To effectively test a fixed pin, you really need a ham-mer. Give the piton a light tap—it should have a high-pitched ring to it, and the hammer should spring off the piton. If you don't have a hammer,

Pitons (left to right): Knifeblade, horizontal, angle

An angle piton, driven all the way to the eye—a good placement

the best test is to clip a sling into it and give it a vigorous yank in the direction you'll be loading it. You can also tap it with a carabiner or small rock. Over time, pitons suffer from the vagaries of thermal expansion and contraction, particularly in winter, as water expands when it freezes, prying and loosening the piton. Often a piton can be easily plucked out with your fingers after only a few seasons. If utilizing fixed pitons as part of your toprope anchor system, use them with skepticism—and always back them up.

Bolts

The most common fixed anchor is a 2-bolt anchor. Some knowledge of the history, characteristics, and specifications of bolts used for rock climbing will improve your ability to assess the reliability of bolt anchors.

In the 1960s and 1970s, bolts were placed by hand drilling—an arduous process where a drill bit was inserted into a drill holder, then a hammer was used to pound on the holder to painstakingly drill into the rock. Once the hole was deep enough, a bolt, with a hanger attached, was hammered into the hole. The most common bolt during that era was the ubiquitous ¼-inch contraction bolt, called the Rawl Drive, manufactured by the Rawl Company and designed for the construction industry for anchoring in masonry or concrete. A contraction bolt has a split shaft that is wider than the diameter of the hole. When pounded into the hole, the two bowed shaft pieces are forced to straighten slightly, contracting under tension in the hole. This works fine for hard granite, but in soft rock, like sandstone, the split shaft doesn't really contract all that much, and there is little tension to keep it in the hole, resulting in very weak pullout strength (i.e., pulling straight out on the bolt).

Another problem with ¼-inch bolts is that they came in various lengths, some as short as ¾-inch long, and once placed in the rock, there was no way for future climbers to determine the length of the bolt merely by inspection.

There are two basic styles of ¼-inch Rawl Drive bolts. The buttonhead design has a mushroom-like head and is pounded into the hole with the hanger pre-attached. The threaded Rawl Drive has threads with a nut on the end to hold the hanger in place, a weaker configuration since the threads can decrease the shear strength of the shaft if the hanger is at the level of the threads. But more significantly, the threaded design has a serious flaw: If you pull straight out, the bolt hanger will only be as strong as the holding power of the nut on the threads, a dangerous problem if the nut is at the very end of the threads.

The shear strength on a brand-new ¼-inch Rawl Drive bolt is roughly 2,000 pounds, but the problem with contraction bolts is not shear strength but pullout strength, which varies drastically depending on the quality and hardness of the rock. In very soft sandstone the pullout strength of a ¼-inch contraction bolt is extremely low, rendering the bolt unsafe.

The buttonhead Rawl Drive bolts were also sold in 5⁄16-inch diameters, these being far more reliable as long as they were placed in good, hard, fine-grained granite. The 5⁄16-inch buttonhead, for example, has shear and pullout strength in excess of 4,000 pounds, and for many years it was the bolt of choice for first ascensionists who were hand-drilling bolts. The 5⁄16-inch buttonhead Rawl Drive has been discontinued, but the 3⁄8-inch buttonhead is still on the market, with a shear strength of 7,000 pounds and a pullout strength of more than 4,000 pounds in the best granite.

Probably the most disconcerting problem associated with bolts from the ¼-inch era is not the bolts themselves but the hangers. During that time, hangers made for rock climbing were manufactured primarily by the SMC company. Thankfully, the hangers are easily identified, as the "SMC" brand is stamped on them. There were two series of hangers—one good, one very bad. The bad hangers were nicknamed the SMC "death hanger," since some of them failed under body weight after only a few seasons of exposure to the elements. These hangers are identifiable by a distinctive corrosive discoloration—a yellowish or bronze tint—whereas the "good" SMC hangers, made from stainless steel, show no signs of corrosion or rust and still appear silvery bright, even after thirty years. Another noticeable difference is in the thickness of the hangers—the bad hangers are roughly the thickness of a dime; the good ones, the thickness of a quarter. A definitive indicator to identify good versus bad SMC hanger is in the SMC stamp itself. On the old, bad hangers, "SMC" is stamped horizontally

The infamous ¼-inch threaded Rawl Drive contraction bolt, complete with the SMC "death hanger." This ticking time bomb was removed and replaced from a route on Suicide Rock, California.

Buttonhead Rawl Drive contraction bolt comparison (left to right): 3⁄8-, 5⁄16-, and ¼-inch sizes

Learn the difference between these two hangers—one good, one very bad. They were manufactured by the SMC company and stamped "SMC" on the hanger. The one on the left is the infamous "SMC death hanger"—slightly thinner and, since it was made of carbon steel, corroded with a yellowish, bronze, or rust tint. The "good" SMC hanger on the right is made of stainless steel and shows no signs of corrosion, even after thirty years on the rock. Another identifying feature is that on the "bad" hanger "SMC" is stamped horizontally, while on the good hanger, "SMC" is stamped vertically.

A ⁵⁄₁₆-inch buttonhead Rawl contraction bolt with "good" SMC hanger. In a good placement in solid granite, these bolts were rated at more than 4,000 pounds shear strength when brand-new. But since they're made of carbon steel, corrosion over time has become a big problem, and now they're considered suspect.

on the hanger; on the new, good hangers, "SMC" is stamped vertically on the hanger.

Another dangerous relic from the 1970s is the Leeper hanger. More than 9,000 of these hangers were manufactured by Ed Leeper of Colorado and subsequently recalled because of stress corrosion problems with the metal, which rusted badly since it was not made of stainless steel. These hangers are easily identifiable due to their strange geometric shape and rusty condition.

In the 1980s sport climbing was ushered into the United States, and climbers began to place bolts on rappel using cordless rotary hammer power drills. Since these bolts would now have to absorb numerous falls, climbers began to look for the strongest bolts available, and the standard became ⅜-inch diameter for good, solid rock (like granite) and ½-inch diameter for softer rock (like sandstone)—standards that are still prevalent today.

Although there are numerous types of bolts used in rock climbing today, the gold standard has long been the "5-piece Rawl" expansion bolt (now sold as the Dewalt Power-Bolt). This expansion bolt has a shaft with a hex head on one end and threads on the other end (the end that goes in the hole), with a cone-shaped piece screwed onto the threads. The shaft has a two-part split sleeve, and as the hex head is tightened the cone climbs up the threads and under the sleeves, which presses the sleeves outward, "expanding" the bolt in the hole. The more you tighten it, the wider the sleeve gets. The performance and strength of the bolt relies, to a great extent, on two things: the tolerance (diameter) of the hole and the strength of the rock itself. In good rock, the ⅜-inch Power-Bolt is rated at more than 7,000 pounds shear strength, with a pullout strength of roughly 5,000 pounds.

Since these bolts are really designed for the construction business, the Dewalt company lists strength ratings based on the density of the concrete they are placed in. Concrete is given a psi (pounds per square inch) rating. For example, "2,000 psi concrete" means that if you took a square inch of concrete, it would take a weight of 2,000 pounds to crush it. Hard, dense granite is analogous to 6,000 psi concrete, and soft sandstone is more like 1,000 psi concrete.

Once a bolt has been installed, it's impossible to see what's going on beneath the surface (like with the length of the bolt), and all you'll see is the head of the bolt, again making identification of the type of bolt more difficult.

If you'd like to educate yourself, peruse "mechanical anchors" on the Dewalt company website (anchors.dewalt.com); you'll get an excellent tutorial on the various types of bolts and how strong they are in different rock types.

Even if you're not an expert in mechanical engineering or in identifying bolt design and type, you should know what to watch for when inspecting a bolt anchor. An obvious red flag is rust. SMC "death hangers," Leeper hangers, aluminum hangers, homemade hangers, and any bolt or hanger with obvious signs of corrosion should never be trusted. Look closely and identify the diameter of the bolt. A ⅜-inch-diameter bolt has become the minimum standard, along with a stainless steel hanger. A bolt with threads and a nut holding the hanger in place is generally not as strong as the hex head types.

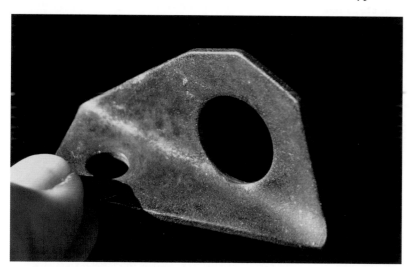

The recalled Leeper hanger can easily be identified by its unique shape and rusty condition.

Bad corrosion on a ⅜-inch-diameter threaded Rawl Drive bolt with a badly corroded Leeper hanger to match

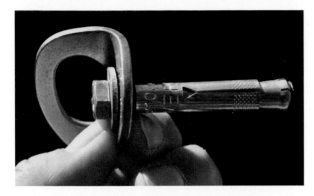

The ⅜-inch-diameter Power-Bolt expansion bolt with a stainless steel hanger has become the minimum standard for climbing anchor bolts.

The ⅜-inch-diameter stainless steel Power-Bolt expansion bolt matched with a stainless hanger is considered the minimum standard. In good granite these bolts rate at around 7,000 pounds shear strength and 5,000 pounds pull-out strength. Most climbers who replace old bolts now use the ½-inch-diameter stainless steel Power-Bolt (10,000 lb. shear strength). If you're installing bolts, use a stainless steel bolt matched with a stainless steel hanger to avoid any corrosion problems or reactions between mixed metals.

A ⅜-inch threaded wedge expansion bolt, another commonly seen bolt. Check to make sure the nut is tightly screwed down to secure the hanger on these bolts.

A spinner is a bolt placement where the hanger moves freely, and you can spin it around the bolt in a circle. Here, the hole wasn't drilled deeply enough, so when the ⁵⁄₁₆-inch button head was pounded in, it hit the back of the hole before the buttonhead came up flush against the hanger.

The rock should not show cracks emanating from the bolt placement—a more common problem with contraction bolts than expansion bolts.

In a good placement, the hanger should be flush against the rock and should not budge or be deformed in any way. A "spinner" is a bolt that protrudes enough so that the hanger can be easily spun around 360 degrees. This generally means that when the bolt was installed, the hole was not drilled deeply enough, and the bolt contacted the bottom of the hole before the hanger could be drawn flush against the rock.

If the bolt wiggles slightly when you pull on it or the hanger is loose, and the bolt has a hex head or a nut on threads, tightening the bolt with a wrench may help, but most likely the bolt has a problem that can't be fixed. If, while trying to tighten it you feel no increasing resistance, and it won't tighten any further, then the bolt has serious problems—usually this means the tolerance (diameter) of the hole is too big for the bolt or the rock is too soft.

As someone who has replaced many bolts over the years, I can tell you that any ¼-inch bolt should

All these old bolts at Joshua Tree were replaced with brand-new stainless steel hardware, courtesy of the ASCA.

be considered suspect, particularly in less than perfect rock. I've plucked out many ¼-inch contraction bolts that came out with about the same resistance as a nail being pulled out of plywood. To replace a ¼-inch bolt, the best method is to pry it out of its hole, then redrill the same hole to a ½-inch diameter and install a ½-inch-diameter stainless steel Power-Bolt (10,000 lb. shear strength) with a stainless steel hanger. I like to paint the hanger (before I install it) the same color as the rock so that the bolt is visually unobtrusive. It's a good feeling to replace a ticking time bomb with a solid anchor that will last a lifetime.

The American Safe Climbing Association (ASCA) has been very active in donating the necessary (and expensive) hardware to climbers, like myself, who take on the task of upgrading unsafe bolt anchors with modern, stainless steel bolts and hangers. If you'd like to support and donate to the ASCA, you can contact them at safeclimbing.org.

Toprope Anchor Systems

The SRENE Principle

The SRENE principle is a simple, easy-to-remember acronym used for evaluating a toprope anchor system. SRENE stands for **S**olid, **R**edundant, **E**qualized, and **N**o **E**xtension.

"Solid" refers to the structural integrity of the rock, from a macro to micro rock evaluation. A macro evaluation is the big picture: Is the crack system you're using a "crack in the planet" or a loose flake or block? Microstructure refers to the quality of the rock inside the crack: Is it hollow, rotten, or flaky?

"Redundancy" means there is no place in the anchor system where you are relying on any one single piece of equipment, be it a strand of cord, sling, or carabiner—in other words, there is always a backup. For bolt anchors the minimum would be two bolts, preferably ⅜-inch diameter. For toprope gear anchors utilizing nuts and camming devices, a good minimum number—and the industry standard for professional guides—is three pieces of gear. Clipping a climbing rope into the anchor system's master point with a single, locking carabiner would not be redundant. With regard to rock structure, if the integrity of the rock is at all in question, using two different rock structures (e.g., two different crack systems) would add redundancy.

"Equalization" means that when the load is applied to the master point on the anchor system, the weight is distributed onto all the various components in the anchor. An anchor can be pre-equalized, which means the system is tied off to accept a force in one specific direction (most often the case in toproping), or self-equalizing, meaning the anchor is rigged to adjust to loading within a range of direction changes.

"No Extension" means that if any one piece in the anchor fails, there will not be any significant amount of slack that develops before the load can be transferred to the remaining pieces. This is a key concept to remember when rigging toprope anchors that are extended over the edge, as often the anchors are a significant distance from the master point. A good rule of thumb is to limit any extension in your anchor system to no more than half the length of a single-length (24-inch) sling.

Principles of Equalization

Pre-Equalized: The Cordelette System

The cordelette system is a pre-equalized system, meaning that once you tie off the cordelette in the anticipated direction of loading, if the load shifts slightly in any direction, all the load goes onto

Adam Radford prepares a rappel site,
Joshua Tree National Park, California.

one placement (albeit with minimal extension), unlike a self-equalizing system that adjusts with changes in the direction of the loading. For toprope anchor systems, you can, in most cases, readily determine the direction your anchor system will be loaded in, so complex self-equalizing rigs are not required. The cordelette system is essentially a system of backups. If one piece fails, the load transfers instantly to the remaining pieces with minimal shock loading, since the rigging limits extension.

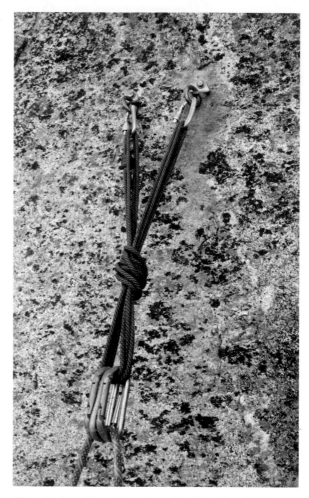

Two bolts pre-equalized with a double-length (48-inch) nylon sling tied with an overhand knot for a toprope setup. The two pear-shaped locking carabiners are opposed and reversed. This simple setup is redundant, equalized in one direction, and rigged for minimal extension. A nylon sling is a better choice than Dyneema for this application, since it has a modicum of stretch and the knot will be easier to untie. If using a Dyneema sling for this purpose, consider using a figure eight instead of an overhand to make it easier to untie after it's weighted.

Simple 2-bolt anchor rigged with a doubled 18-foot 7mm nylon Sterling cordelette. The cordelette is doubled to start with, producing four strands at the master point loop, and the climbing rope is clipped into three oval carabiners opposed and reversed. The bolts have Fixed Ring Anchors, with welded rings rated at 10,000 pounds breaking strength. If you're dealing with old or corroded hardware, it's best to bypass the various quick links, chains, or rings and clip directly into the bolt hangers.

The beauty of the pre-equalized cordelette system is that it is easy to remember and simple to rig. The cordelette is fairly versatile in that it can be used to rig two, three, or four placements. The most common fixed anchor you'll encounter is a 2-bolt anchor. An easy and bomber rig is to start by doubling the cordelette then clipping the doubled strand into both bolts with locking carabiners. Pull down between the bolts, gather all the strands together, and tie a figure eight loop. This gives you four strands of cord at the master point.

To rig three or four placements, clip the cordelette into all the placements, then pull down between the pieces and gather all the loops together. I like to clip a carabiner into all the gathered loops and pull in the anticipated loading direction, then tie a figure eight knot with the carabiner attached to help even out all the strands. If you find yourself coming up a bit short on enough length

Demonstration of pre-equalized cordelette with three anchor placements, tied with a 7mm nylon cordelette. A clove hitch has been tied to the top left piece to keep the double fisherman's knot away from the end loops. This is a simple and effective rig as long as the direction of load is predetermined, which is most often the case when toproping.

Four-piece anchor pre-equalized with 6mm Sterling PowerCord cordelette. The two locking carabiners are opposed and reversed.

to tie off all the loops with a figure eight, an over-hand knot will take up less cord; even though it's a slightly weaker knot, this is not a factor since you'll have at least three or four loops at your master point. Another trick is to take a regular length (24-inch) sling and clip it into the piece that's furthest away from you—this will give you more length to work with on the cordelette.

Rigging a Cordelette

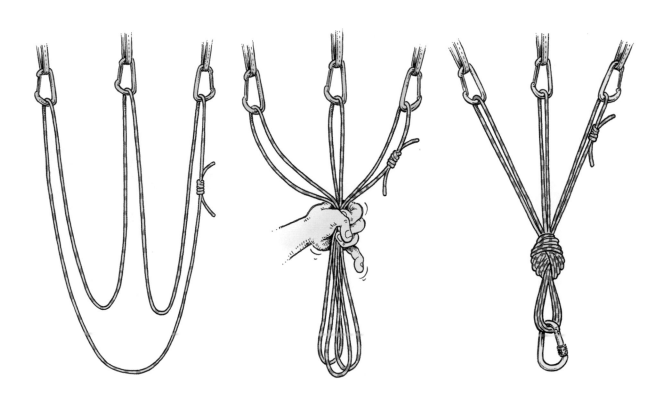

An 18- to 20-foot-long cordelette is usually long enough to equalize three or four anchor points, as long as they are not spaced too far apart. Use a sling or two if necessary to get all the carabiners you'll be clipping into within a workable range. Clip a single strand of the cordelette into each cara-biner, then pull down between the pieces and gather the loops (with three pieces you'll have three loops). Clipping a carabiner into the loops before you tie the knot will make it easier to equalize all the strands. Tie a figure eight knot to create your master point, which should be roughly 3 to 4 inches in diameter. If you don't have enough cord to tie a figure eight, an overhand knot takes up less cord.

Here a 7mm nylon cordelette has been untied and used in its full length. Many professional guides tie their cordelettes with a knot that can be easily untied so that, if necessary, they can use the full length as shown here. A good knot to use to tie your cordelette into its original loop is a flat overhand (make sure the tails are at least 8 inches long, or back it up with a second overhand tied right on top of the first one) or a figure eight bend, tied with the tails at least 3 inches long. The figure eight bend is a much stronger knot, but it's more difficult to untie.

The drawback of the cordelette system (left) is that if the direction of the anticipated load changes, one piece in the anchor takes all the load (right). Think of the cordelette system as a system of back-ups: If the one piece that is loaded fails, the load goes onto the next piece with relatively minimal extension in the system. For toproping anchors, since the load on the anchor system is relatively low, the cordelette system has the advantage of being easy to use and simple to rig, negating any potential for shock loading.

Self-Equalizing Systems

THE SLIDING X

The sliding X (aka magic X) is a simple way to equalize two anchor points with a sling, creating a mini–anchor system that adjusts as the load shifts in direction. In scrutinizing the overall anchor system, if I use a sliding X between two pieces with one sling, I count this as only one placement as far as redundancy is concerned, because it is only one sling. However, by equalizing two placements that can adjust to slight shifts in direction, you create one more inherently bomber piece.

If using the sliding X with a long sling (like a sewn, 48-inch double-length sling), you can minimize extension by tying overhand knots just above the clip-in point. This allows the system to adjust, but limits any extension if one piece fails.

To set up a simple self-equalizing anchor system from two bolts, you can use two single-length slings together with a sliding X, creating a redundant rig with minimal extension.

Rigging a Sliding X

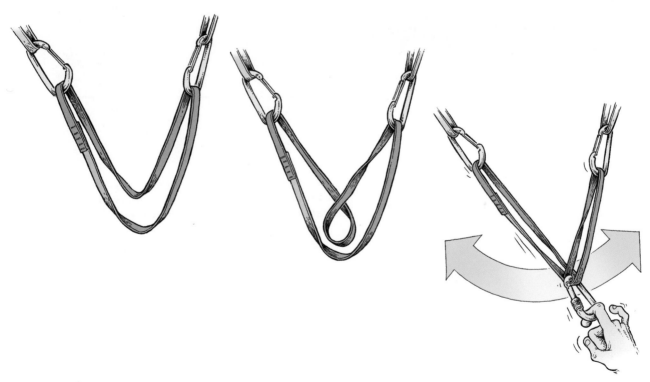

Using a single sling, you can create a self-equalizing system that adjusts with changes in the direction of loading. Perfect equalization is rarely achieved, since to divide the load equally between two points, both of the angles between the direction of pull and each of the slings leading to their respective anchor points must be identical.

When rigging a sliding X, make sure you clip into the loop you've created by twisting the sling.

When the loops are of unequal length on a sliding X rig, you can limit extension (and potential shock loading) by tying an overhand knot on the longer end, just above the carabiner. But because there is no knot on the locking carabiner side of the sling, this setup lacks redundancy at the master point, since you're relying on single, twisted loop of the sling.

Stacked Xs. In this three-piece anchor, redundancy has been achieved by tying two extension-limiting knots on the purple sling.

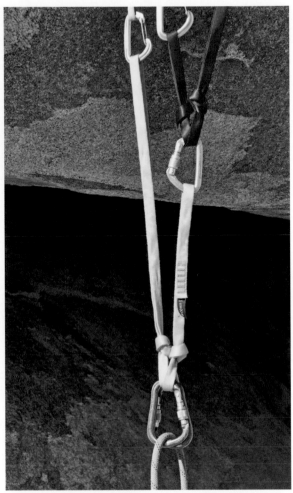

Stacked Xs. By tying two overhand knots on both the red and yellow double-length nylon slings, this three-piece anchor has redundancy and minimal extension throughout the system.

This toprope anchor is self-equalizing but lacks redundancy in three critical elements: in the single, rewoven 1-inch tubular nylon sling; the single yellow cordelette; and the single locking carabiner that connects them. While plenty strong, the issue here is not one of strength but of redundancy. Lack of redundancy is a problem for unmonitored toprope anchors like this one, particularly if it's being heavily used, since the soft nylon cordellete will get abraded over the edge and no one will see it happening. Also, if one of the three pieces were to fail, you'd get some major movement in the red sling, resulting in shock loading the two remaining pieces.

A simple 2-bolt anchor can be rigged with a sliding X using two separate slings and two locking carabiners at the master point for a redundant, self-equalizing system. With a 2-bolt anchor, I always use locking carabiners on the bolt hangers too. The drawback of this rig is that if one bolt were to fail, the system would extend to the length of the slings. As a general rule, limit the maximum extension in your anchor system to half the length of a single-length (24-inch) sling, which is what we have here.

A 2-bolt toprope anchor rigged with a sliding X and extension-limiting knots. By using a double-length (48-inch) nylon sling tied with two overhand knots, the sling itself becomes redundant at the master point, since it has two loops of webbing.

THE QUAD

The quad is a great system to use for equalizing 2-bolt toprope anchors. It gives you near-perfect equalization with minimal extension and great strength. To rig the quad, start by doubling your cordelette, then grab the middle with your fist. Tie an overhand knot on each side of your fist, and you're ready to rig. Clip the double-strand loops into the bolts with locking carabiners, then clip only three of the four strands at the master point, leaving one loop outside your master point carabiners. This ensures that if one bolt fails, you are clipped into a pocket on the master point.

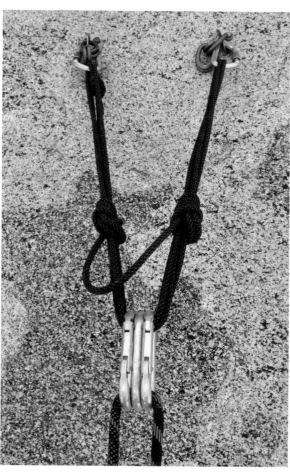

A 2-bolt anchor rigged with a 7mm cordelette and the quad system. The cordelette is clipped directly to the bolt hangers with locking carabiners, bypassing the cheap hardware store lap links (which are rated only at around 1,000 lb.).

Detail of quad rig master point with three ovals opposed and reversed

Detail of quad rig with two locking carabiners opposed and reversed

Quad rig using Sterling 6mm PowerCord and three steel ovals for a toprope setup

THE EQUALETTE

The equalette rig gives you four strands, or "arms," running from the master point to the various pieces in your anchor matrix. These four arms can be tied to the pieces with figure eights, clove hitches, or

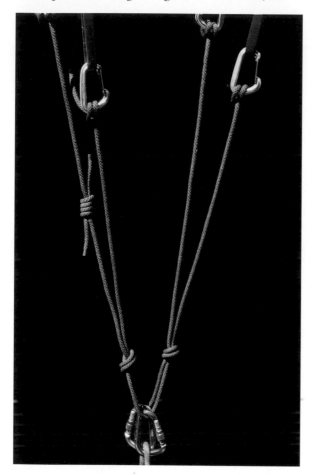

The equalette rigged with a 7mm nylon corde-lette. This is a versatile system to use for equal-izing three or four placements, giving you re-dundancy, equalization, and no extension. The only drawback is in its complexity and the fact that it does not have one singular master point to clip into. Here the equalette is rigged to four placements, using the various "arms" of the cordelette attached with clove hitches for easy adjustment.

double loop knots like the double loop eight or double loop bowline.

To tie an equalette rig, form a U shape with your cordelette and grab the bottom of the U, positioning the fisherman's knot on the cordelette about 18 inches away from the bottom of the U. Tie an overhand knot on both sides of your fist, about 10 inches apart.

At the master point, you'll have two separate loops. Clip into each loop with a separate locking carabiner.

Detail of the equalette master point using two locking carabiners opposed and reversed

Vectors

A vector is a quantity that incorporates both direction and magnitude. Picture a tightrope walker balancing out on the middle of a wire. If he weighs 200 pounds, the load at each end where the wire is attached will be roughly 1,000 pounds. Why is this? When two anchor points are equalized, as the angle of the wire, sling, cord, or rope approaches 180 degrees, the forces at the anchor points increase drastically. When the angle is narrow, the load is distributed at around 50 percent to each anchor.

Keep this in mind when you build toprope anchor systems. If the angle between two anchor points reaches 120 degrees, you'll load each anchor at 100 percent. Strive to keep all the angles under 60 degrees so you'll be splitting the load roughly 50/50. A good rule of thumb is to always keep the angles under 90 degrees. Also, avoid rigging a sling between two anchors in a triangular configuration (called the American Triangle), which, even at 90 degrees, places 1.3 times the force at each anchor point. An American Triangle rigged at 120 degrees would almost double the load at each anchor point!

The American Triangle rigged at a rappel anchor. Avoid rigging with a triangle configuration—it adds unnecessary forces to your anchor points. Stick to a V configuration for lower loads.

American Triangle

Load per anchor with 100 lb. of force

Bottom Angle	V Rigging	Triangle Rigging
30 degrees	52 lb.	82 lb.
60 degrees	58 lb.	100 lb.
90 degrees	71 lb.	131 lb.
120 degrees	100 lb.	193 lb.
150 degrees	193 lb.	380 lb.

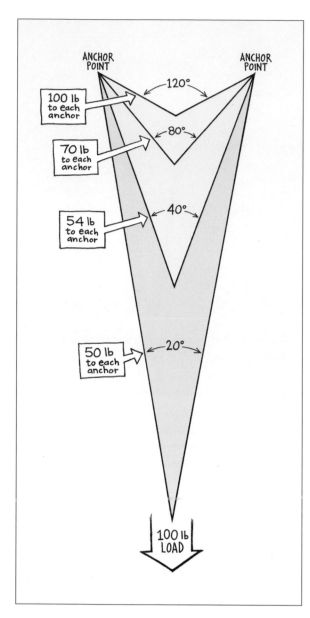

ANCHOR
POINT

ANCHOR
POINT

120°

100 lb
to each
anchor

80°

70 lb
to each
anchor

40°

54 lb
to each
anchor

20°

50 lb
to each
anchor

100 lb
LOAD

This diagram illustrates how a 100-pound load is distributed between two anchor points at various angles. Keep the angle between two anchors as narrow as possible, striving to keep it under 60 degrees. At 120 degrees the load is 100 percent at each anchor! Think of 0 to 60 degrees as ideal, 60 to 90 degrees a caution zone, and over 90 degrees a danger zone.

Redundancy

When NASA studied redundant systems on their spacecraft they theorized that if one particular system had a failure rate of 1 in 1,000, then by backing it up with a redundant system the failure rate (for both to fail) was more like 1 in 1 million (1,000 × 1,000).

When it comes to climbing anchors, it's not quite that simple, but let's agree that redundancy is part of a minimum standard for rock climbing anchors. What redundancy means is this: When you evaluate your anchor from the master point to the various components, there is no place in the anchor system where you're relying on a single element—be it one nut, cam, cord, sling, carabiner, etc.—there is always a backup.

Exceptions to the rule might be a monolithic anchor (like a 2-foot-diameter ponderosa pine tree), but you can still achieve redundancy in the rigging.

While redundancy is important, it does not guarantee a failsafe anchor. You must not lose sight of the most important elements of what constitutes a good anchor: good rock structure and good anchor placements. You should have the ability to quickly and effectively assess any anchor system based on standard assessment criteria. Evaluating redundancy alone does not get you there.

Anchor System Assessment for Gear Anchors

To assess the anchor system, I use a macro-to-micro progression. Don't lose sight of the big picture and get focused on the minutia. Number one is the structural integrity of the rock itself. Without solid rock, no matter how great the individual placements are, a catastrophic failure is possible due to failure of the rock structure. The ideal is the "crack in the planet"—a crack in massive rock that bisects the plane of the rock face at a right angle. Loose blocks, flakes, and cracked rock should all be considered suspect. Be critical in assessing rock

The SRENE Principle

S Solid (Structural Integrity of the Rock)
R Redundant
E Equalized
N No
E Extension

structure—it's literally the foundation your anchor is built upon.

Next, look at the overall anchor rigging. Is it redundant? Is it well equalized, with no extension? A good general rule is to limit the extension in any anchor system to no more than half the length of a single (24-inch) sling. To pass muster, the anchor system must satisfy the SRENE principle in general.

Finally, scrutinize each individual placement, starting with the microstructure of the rock. Are there loose flakes, hollow spots, or any rotten or disintegrating rock within the crack? Then look closely at each individual placement. If it's a nut, does it satisfy the SOS principle (Structure, Orientation, Surface Contact)? If it's a camming device, is it in the manufacturer's recommended range of retraction?

The 12-Point Anchor System Evaluation Rubric

A rubric is a scoring system used to assign quality ratings to a task, or to delineate criteria for assigning a grade or score.

According to Wikipedia, in educational terminology a rubric is "a scoring guide used to evaluate the quality of students' constructed responses."

Merriam-Webster defines a rubric as "a guide listing specific criteria for grading or scoring academic papers, projects, or tests."

During anchor classes, to teach assessment of placements, I often use the traditional rubrics, like the education letter grading system (A+, A-, B+, B, B-, etc.) or rate placements on a scale of 0 to 10 (10 being perfection).

The 12-point anchor system assessment rule was developed decades ago by rock climbing instructors at the National Outdoor Leadership School (NOLS) but was never widely adopted.

It works like this: For an anchor to pass evaluation, it must achieve a total score of 12 points or more.

Here are some examples of how points are assigned:

- **12 points:** A true monolithic natural anchor, like a huge tree or block
- **12-point tree:** Must be live, deeply rooted in soil, with a minimum trunk diameter of 12 inches at 2 feet up from its base
- **12-point granite block:** Must be as big as a full-size refrigerator, resting lengthwise on a flat surface
- **6 points:** A modern, well-placed, ⅜-inch diameter bolt with no signs of corrosion, in high-quality rock
- **4 points:** A larger cam or nut (e.g., Black Diamond Camalot size 0.5 and up (12–14 kN) or Black Diamond Stopper size 6–12 (10 kN), or Black Diamond Hex size 4–11 (10 kN)
- **3 points:** A medium-size cam or nut (e.g., Black Diamond Camalot size 0.3–0.4 (8–9 kN) or Black Diamond Stopper size 3–5 (5–6 kN)

In general, for rigging toprope anchors, you won't want any tiny pieces (e.g., Stoppers size 1–3 or micro cams ½ inch and smaller) in your anchor system. These are tools for leading and aid climbing, so a piece rated at 1 or 2 points shouldn't come into play.

Using the 12-point rubric, you must not lose sight of the overall assessment criteria for an anchor system: How is the rock structure? Do the individual placements meet evaluation standard requirements? Is the anchor rigging redundant? With no extension?

Remember, the 12-point rubric is just another assessment tool in your toolbox, not a standalone assessment guideline.

The 25 kN Anchor System Evaluation Rubric

This is another concept I use to evaluate the strength of a toprope anchor. The concept is this: The strength of your anchor placements should add up to at least 25 kN. For example: 2 large nuts and 1 large cam = 34 kN (10 kN + 10 kN + 14 kN).

To use this concept in the field, you'll have to learn and memorize the breaking strength of your gear, gleaned from the manufacturer's hangtags and websites, which is the theoretical breaking strength in the best rock/placement.

Going through this exercise is a learning experience and a valuable tool that will get you thinking about how strong the components on your rack are. It's common sense: Larger pieces are generally stronger than smaller ones, but some of the breaking strengths may surprise you.

During guides courses, I often ask a student, "How strong is that cord you have there?" The answer is usually "I don't know." "Is it nylon or some other high-tech cord?" I ask them. Again, "I don't know" is usually the answer. Well, there's a big difference between 6mm nylon cord (usually rated around 8 kN/1,798 lb. tensile breaking strength) and 6mm high-tech cord (like New England Tech cord, 22 kN/almost 5,000 lb. tensile breaking strength).

The 25 kN number gives you a healthy safety margin (more than 3 to 1), since in a toprope situation you'll only be able to generate maybe 4 kN of force on the anchor in a worst-case scenario of a toprope fall with a bunch of slack in the rope if you're using a dynamic rope, and roughly double that (8 kN) if you're using a low-stretch rope with an tightly anchored belayer and a device that locks off statically, like a Grigri.

One thing you'll notice using this evaluation is that to get to 25 kN you'll usually need at least three gear placements, which is the industry standard for rock climbing instructors rigging toprope anchors.

Using 25 kN (5,620 lb.) as your minimum gives you plenty of leeway, allowing for variables like less than perfect rock quality and less than perfect rock structure. It will serve as a tool to help you evaluate your overall anchor system's holding capability, but don't overlook the other necessary assessment criteria.

What Is a Kilonewton? (kN)

A newton was named for, you guessed it, Sir Isaac Newton in recognition of his groundbreaking work: Newton's Second Law of Motion. A newton measures mass in motion.

One newton is the force required to accelerate 1 kilogram of mass at the rate of 1 meter per second squared, or roughly the force of gravity acting on a small mass (like an apple) on planet Earth. One kilonewton is equal to 1,000 newtons.

To wrap my head around this concept, I like to think of it in terms of pounds and how much load a piece can sustain. One kN is equal to 101.97 kilograms of load; 1 kilogram is equal to 2.205 pounds, so 1 kN is equal to 224.8 pounds of force. So a sling that's rated to 22 kN could theoretically hold 2,243 kilograms (4,946 lb.). It's not that simple, however, since a kN rating signifies the maximum impact force the sling can withstand, which is a force of gravity rating (force = mass × acceleration), but it's easier for me to grasp the concept that, yes, I could hang my car from that sling.

Remember, the 25 kN rule does not work independently of a SRENE Principle assessment, since it doesn't matter how many pieces you've placed in the rock if they're placed in bad rock structure, like in a loose flake or beneath a detached block. It's still paramount to evaluate rock structure (macro to micro) and assess that all your cams are in the recommended range of retraction and all your nuts satisfy the SOS evaluation principle.

To convert kN to pounds of force in a simple calculation, multiply kN × 224.8.

25 kN is roughly 5,620 pounds of force.

The Joshua Tree System

Joshua Tree National Park is a vast area, with hundreds of crags to choose from. The setups can be time-consuming and gear intensive because most anchors require gear placements set well back from the cliff edge, and bolted anchors are a rarity. Out of necessity we developed a system to rig toprope anchors that is both efficient and redundant, using a length of low-stretch rope. I call it the Joshua Tree System, and I can vouch for its efficiency—it's the system we've used for more than thirty-five years in my climbing school on countless toprope setups.

For your rigging rope, I'd recommend either 10mm or 10.5mm diameter. For most situations a 60-foot length will suffice. My favorite rigging rope is the Sterling Safety Pro, which is EN 1891 certified, with a stretch of about 4 percent in a toprope fall situation. This rope handles well and has good abrasion resistance. It can also be used for fixed lines, tethering, rappelling, and toproping. You don't want to use a dynamic rope for toprope rigging, since its stretch will make it seesaw back and forth over edges, and you don't want to use a low-stretch rope for leading.

To rig the Joshua Tree System, visualize a V configuration, with two separate anchors at the top of the V and your master point at the bottom, or point, of the V. The master point is tied with a BHK ("big

honking knot"), which is essentially an overhand knot tied on a doubled bight, which gives you two-loop redundancy at the master point.

In the Joshua Tree System, we call the rigging rope an "extension," or "extendo," rope. The two separate strands of rope that run from the master point to anchors A and B are the "legs" of the extension rope.

Ideally, the angle of the V should be less than 60 degrees—and at least less than 90 degrees. Once you have determined where the climb is and where you want your master point, picture the V in your mind and begin to set your anchors. If using natural anchors, it could be as simple as two trees. If you climb at areas with many trees at the clifftop, you're in luck; the Joshua Tree System will simplify your rigging. All you need is the rigging rope itself—no slings or cordelettes required. Tie one end of your rigging rope around one tree with a simple bowline. Run the rope over the edge and tie a BHK. I usually weight a bight of rope with a few carabiners and let it dangle about 4 feet over the edge, knowing that when I pull it back up and tie the BHK, the master point will end up about 4 feet higher, which is the length of doubled bight taken up by tying the BHK. Then tie around the second tree with a bowline with a bight, and you're done.

With gear anchors the combinations are endless, but a good minimum is at least three gear placements. Most of my setups tend to end up with two gear placements on each end of the V. If you learn to tie double loop knots, you can eliminate the need for slings and cordelettes in most situations.

For safety as you approach the cliff edge, protect yourself by tethering with a double-length (48-inch) $^{11}\!/_{16}$-inch nylon sling. Pick the leg of the V you feel is stronger or the one that's redundant (two pieces) and tether to that strand by tying a klemheist knot around it and attaching the other end of the sling to your harness belay loop with a locking carabiner. A nylon sling is preferable to a Spectra or Dyneema one, since nylon grips better on the

Tying the BHK ("Big Honking Knot")

Start by taking a doubled bight about 4 feet long.

Tie an overhand knot on all four strands.

Thread the two loops back through the loop you've created . . .

. . . or incorporate the loop into the master point carabiners.

Tether detail. If you're working at the cliff's edge, protect yourself. This climber has rigged his BHK master point, all the while protected with a personal tether—a double-length nylon sling. He has secured one end of the sling to his harness to a locking carabiner; the other end is attached to the rigging rope via a klemheist knot.

Overview of the Joshua Tree System. The left "leg" of the extension rope is attached with a double-loop bowline to two cams; the right leg is clove hitched to a single, bomber cam. A BHK is tied for the master point, with three opposed and reversed oval carabiners ready for the climbing rope.

Close-up of the master point using a BHK and three oval carabiners with the gates opposed and reversed

Another version of the Joshua Tree System. Here, both legs have two cams equalized with sliding Xs—an elaborate rig, but one that fully adjusts to any shift, however minor, in the direction of pull. In most setups I prefer to use double-loop knots; it's more efficient, and since I know the direction my anchor will be loaded in, I'm not worried about drastic vector changes.

friction hitch and has a bit of stretch, whereas Spectra or Dyneema is slicker, static (like a wire cable), and has virtually no stretch. Now you can slide the klemheist knot up and down the rigging rope to safeguard yourself as you work near the edge. Tie a BHK (see page 126) so that your master point dangles just over the lip of the cliff edge, positioned directly above your chosen climb. Attach your climbing rope with carabiners (either two opposed and reversed locking or three opposed and reversed ovals) and run the rope back to anchor B, attaching it with a clove hitch to a locking carabiner. This will allow you to adjust the tension and fine-tune the equalization. Use edge protectors at the lip to protect your rope from abrasion and cutting if sharp edges are present.

The Joshua Tree System rigged with two double-loop figure eights. The climber is tethered with a double-length nylon sling attached to the rigging rope with a klemheist knot and connected to his belay loop with a locking carbiner.

Unmonitored Anchor Systems

Make sure the extension rope is not resting over sharp edges at the lip of the cliff. This setup is an "unmonitored" anchor system, which means that once it is rigged, you'll be at the base and not able to watch what is happening at the anchor—like the extension rope abrading over an edge. Take special care to prevent this by padding the edge (a pack or rope bag will work) or, better yet, using commercially made edge protectors.

Toprope all day long with your extension rope rubbing on a sharp edge, and you'll end up with a seriously abraded rope like this one.

A commercially made edge protector, like this one sold by Petzl, is a wise investment. Attach it to your rigging rope with a friction hitch.

Toprope setup using the Joshua Tree System on rock horns. The top horn is tied with a simple bowline, backed up with half a double fisherman's knot. The bottom horn is tied using a bowline with a bight, backed up with an overhand. The master point is tied with a BHK. This is a great system to use on two trees.

If you learn to tie double-loop knots like the double-loop figure eight and double-loop bowline, along with the in-line figure eight, you'll be able to eliminate many slings and cordelettes from your anchor system and become more efficient in your rigging. For example, when using the Joshua Tree System, I often start with two bomber pieces at the end of one leg on my extension rope then equalize them with a double-loop knot, thus eliminating the need for slings or cordelettes. As I move toward the edge and perhaps find more anchor placements, I use the in-line eight to equalize these pieces to the system. The double-loop knots and in-line eight are mandatory for those who wish to become master riggers!

Making the Transition from Rigging to Rappelling

If you decide to rappel to the base, you will need to transition from your extension rope to your rappel rope. Slide the klemheist knot on your personal tether down one leg of the extension rope (pick what you consider to be the stronger leg) until you approach the edge. Before you get to the edge, pull up your doubled rappel rope, rig your rappel device, and back it up with an autoblock. Slide the klemheist knot down until it's just on top of the BHK.

Make the transition over the edge, using the extension rope for balance, and until you've weighted your rappel system. Double-check everything before removing your personal tether, then proceed to rappel.

Using the Rigging Rope as a Tether

Using your rigging rope as a tether is very useful in situations where just approaching the edge may be unduly hazardous without protection, or if you'd like to make a reconnaissance to an exposed cliff

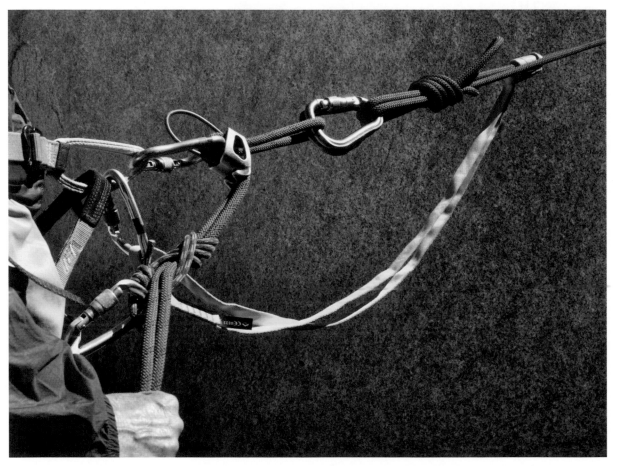

Transition rig detail. If you know you'll be rappelling, don't make your BHK loop too long, since you'll need to get around it without your tether becoming tight. Before you unclip and remove your tether, weight your rappel system and double-check everything. Make sure your autoblock is engaged and not up against your rappel device, which would keep it from grabbing the rope properly.

edge to look down and identify the climb you want to set up. You can rappel down the fixed line using a Grigri, then ascend back up the line using the Grigri as a progress capture device, pulling up slack on the brake side as you ascend. The rope tether is also useful on sport climbing cliffs to approach a bolted sport climbing anchor, which in most cases will be at or below the edge of the cliff. The main safety concern when using a fixed line tether that doesn't reach the ground is the danger of rappelling off the end of the rope, so ALWAYS TIE A STOPPER KNOT IN THE END OF YOUR RIGGING ROPE.

V with a Tether

A variation of the Joshua Tree System, which I call a "V with a tether," utilizes the basic V-rigging configuration of the Joshua Tree System combined with a rope tether coming off the same anchor at the end of one leg of the V.

This system will come in handy if you foresee a very awkward edge transition from rigging to rappelling, or in a situation where the area you'll be working at near the edge is very exposed in sloping terrain. Where it really works well is a situation where you've set an anchor (serving as the anchor on the end of one leg of your V) well back from the cliff edge, but your next anchor (for the other leg of the V) is in a precariously exposed position at the edge or over the edge of the cliff.

To use the V with a tether method, start by building an initial anchor. This should be a bona fide SRENE, 12-point rubric, 25 kN anchor, not just a single piece of gear, since you'll be rappelling on this anchor to the cliff edge—and over the cliff edge if you're rappelling to the base. After building the anchor, measure a length of rigging rope for your tether long enough to go well over the cliff's edge; if you're going to rig a toprope and transition to a rappel to the base on your toprope, measure your tether to be at least 10 feet longer than where your toprope master point will be. Tie

Instructor Erin Guinn rappelling on a rope tether with a Grigri at Joshua Tree. If you're using a rope tether, always tie a stopper knot in the end of the rope to start with. If you take your brake hand off the rope, tie an overhand loop as a backup knot as shown here. If the rope slips through the Grigri (as it will when unweighted) the knot will jam.

Instructor Wills Young using the "V with a tether" rigging configuration at Joshua Tree. His rope tether is connected to a 2-bolt anchor as is one leg of the V. The other leg of the V is connected to a three-piece gear anchor. There is a stopper knot tied in the end of his rope tether, and he has just tied an overhand loop as a backup to his Grigri so that he can go hands-free to complete the toprope rigging. Always tie a stopper knot in the end of your tether before you start using it.

a stopper knot in the end of your rigging rope, then attach it to your initial anchor's master point with a figure eight of a bight and locking carabiner. Now you can connect yourself to the rope tether with a Grigri. The rope running off the other side of your figure eight on a bight will now serve as one leg of the V on your anchor rigging. Rappel using the Grigri to where you need to go to at the edge and finish your rigging, build an anchor for the other leg of your V, tie a BHK for your master point, and connect your climbing rope to the BHK master point. If you take your brake hand off the rope while working at the edge, tie an overhand knot on the brake hand side to back up the Grigri, since if you unweight the rope it will creep through the Grigri. Remember, when using a rope tether, ALWAYS TIE A STOPPER KNOT IN THE END OF THE ROPE tether to prevent rappelling off the end of the rope!

Now you can either ascend back up the rope tether to your top anchor or make a transition to rappelling down the doubled toprope rope.

Making a transition from rigging to rappelling using a rope tether. Here, the instructor has pre-rigged his rappel device and autoblock backup. He's extended his rappel device by using a double-length (48-inch) $^{11}/_{16}$-inch nylon sling basketed through both tie-in points on his harness, then tied with an overhand knot for redundancy. He will now rappel down on his rope tether until he has fully weighted his rappel system. Before unclipping his Grigri from the tether, he'll double-check everything, making sure, first of all, that the three oval carabiners at the toprope master point are properly opposed and reversed, that the locking carabiner on his rappel device and autoblock are locked, and that his autoblock is grabbing the rope properly.

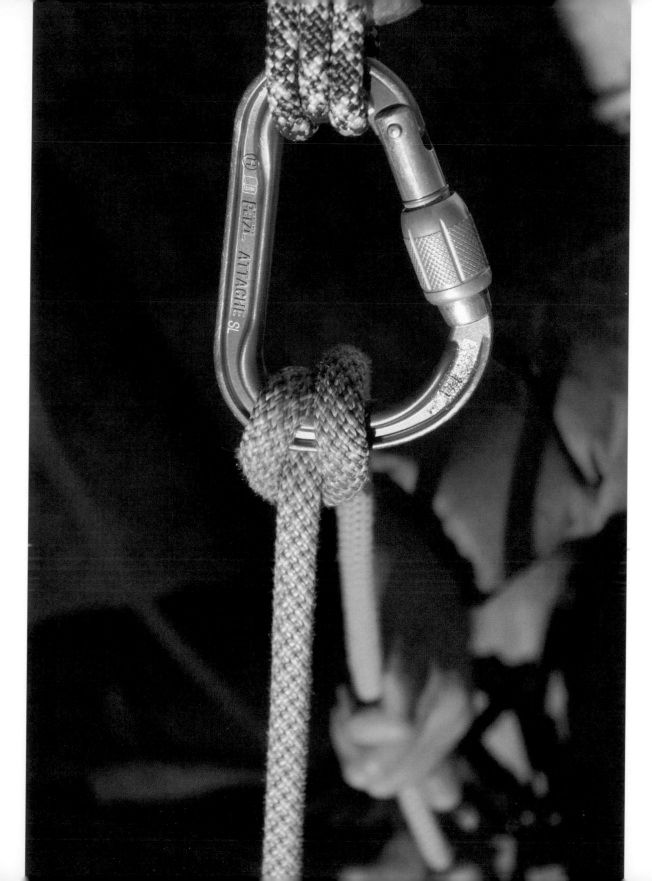

Knots

Overhand loop

Loop Knots

Loop knots are tied by taking two strands of rope (called a bight) and wrapping them back over themselves so that the knot does not slide, or by taking the end of the rope and tying it back over the standing part so the knot does not slide. Loop knots are used to clip the rope into a carabiner or to tie around an object.

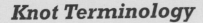

Knot Terminology

Bend: Two ropes tied together by their ends

Bight: Two strands of rope where the rope is doubled back on itself

Load strand: The strand of the rope that bears all the weight

Hitch: A knot that is tied around another object (such as a carabiner or rope)

Standing end: The part of the rope that the end of the rope crosses to form a knot

Tag end: The very end of a rope, or the tail end that protrudes from a knot

Overhand Loop

This is the simplest knot you can tie to form a loop. It requires less rope to tie than the figure eight, which makes it useful on cordelettes when you don't quite have enough length to tie the master point with a figure eight loop. For most applications, however, the figure eight loop is superior because it tests about 10 percent stronger than

Finished overhand loop

the overhand loop and is easier to untie in small-diameter cord.

Figure Eight Follow-Through

This is the standard knot for tying the rope to your harness. It can also be used to tie an anchoring rope around an object like a tree or through a tunnel. Tie it with a 5-inch minimum tail, and tighten all four strands to dress the knot.

A properly tied figure eight follow-through knot

Figure Eight Loop

Another standard climbing knot, the figure eight loop is used for tying off the end of a rope, or for tying a loop in the middle, or "bight," of a rope. It is also commonly referred to as a "figure eight on a bight."

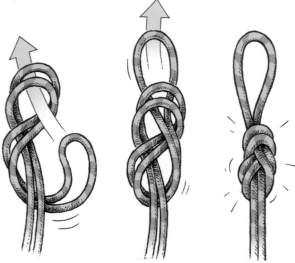

How to tie a figure eight loop

Finished figure eight loop clipped to an anchor

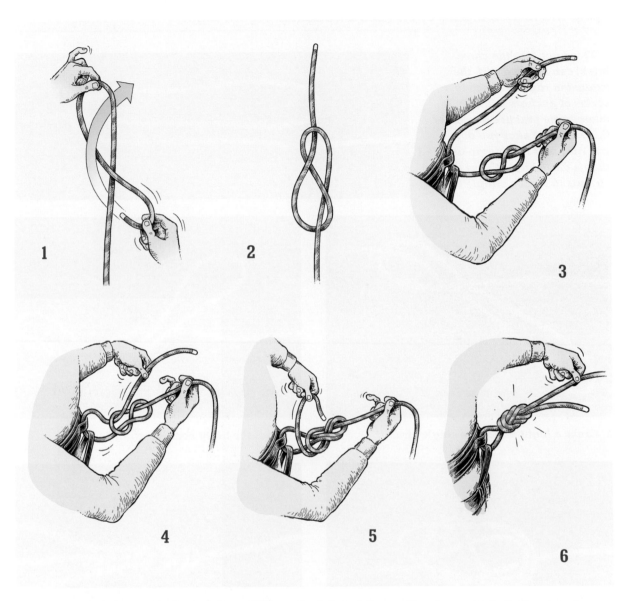

Check your harness manufacturer's guidelines for information on how to properly tie the rope to your harness. For harnesses with belay loops, you generally follow the same path as the belay loop, which goes through two tie-in points on the harness. Tie the figure eight so that its loop is about the same diameter as your belay loop. The figure eight knot does not require a backup knot.

In-Line Figure Eight

Tying the In-line Figure Eight (aka Directional Figure Eight)

1. This knot, like the clove hitch, can be used with the extension rope to attach to a series of anchors in a line. It takes some practice to master this knot, but after you do, you may find it easier to use than a clove hitch. Cross the strands to form a simple loop.

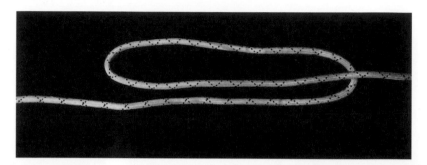

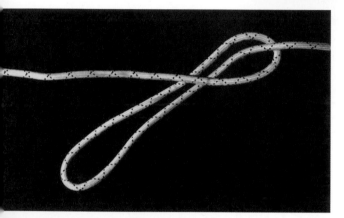

2. Cross a bight under the single strand.

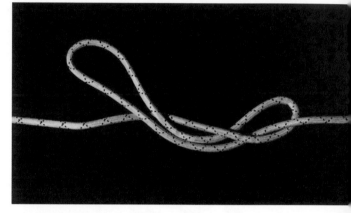

3. Cross the bight over the strand.

4. Thread the bight back through the loop you've just formed.

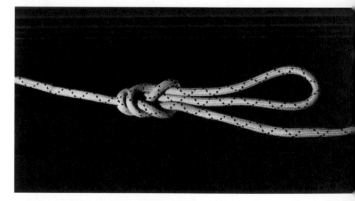

5. Finished in-line figure eight

Bowline

If you were a Boy Scout, you learned this knot with the saying "the rabbit comes up through the hole, around the tree, and back down through the hole." The bowline is very useful to tie the rope around something, like a tree, block of rock, or tunnel in the rock. It is important to note that a bowline knot requires a backup, as weighting and unweighting the knot easily loosens it. Always tie half of a double fisherman's knot to back it up. One advantage of the bowline is this same feature—it is very easy to untie after it has been weighted.

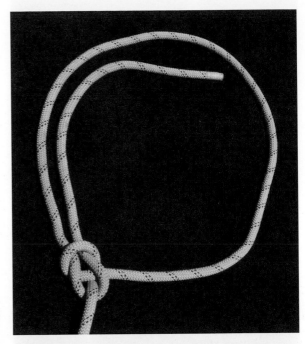

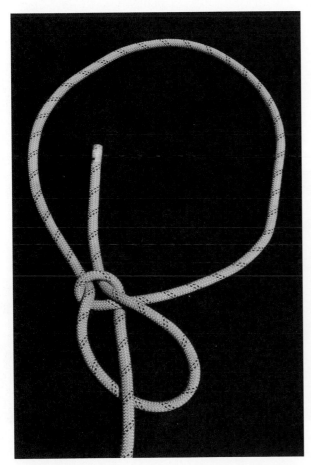

Tying the bowline. The bowline should always be tied with a backup, shown here with half a double fisherman's for the backup knot (final photo).

The bowline knot with fisherman's backup

Rethreaded bowline. Tie a regular bowline, but leave the tail long enough to go all the way back around the object you're tying around, then retrace the start of the knot, like you would on a figure eight follow-through, finishing with a fisherman's backup. This is a great knot to use for tying a rope around a tree or through a tunnel because you end up with two loops, adding strength and redundancy to your rigging.

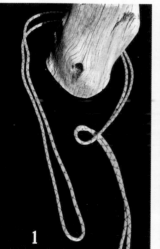
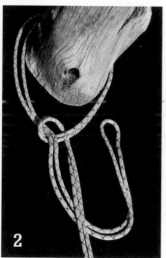
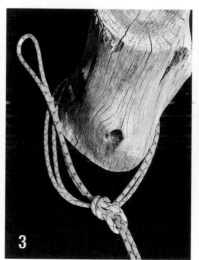

Tying a bowline with a bight (not to be confused with the "bowline on a bight," also known as the double-loop bowline). The big advantage of the bowline with a bight is that you can tie around an object anywhere down the length of the rope without having to pull the tail all the way through. It's essentially the same configuration as a simple bowline but tied with two strands of rope—very useful for tying to trees if using the Joshua Tree System for a toprope rig. Back it up with an overhand (photo 4).

Double-Loop Knots

BHK

BHK is an abbreviation for "big honking knot." Technically, it's an overhand knot tied on a doubled bight. It's commonly used to rig a redundant master point when rigging toprope anchors with an extension rope (using the Joshua Tree System).

Tying a BHK

1. Start with a bight of rope and double it.

2. Tie an overhand knot on all four strands.

3. Thread the two loops back through the single loop you've created . . .

4. . . . or incorporate all three loops into the master point carabiners.

Double-Loop Figure Eight

This knot is very useful for pre-equalizing two anchor points. Note that if the two loops are used together to form a master point, they are not redundant due to the rewoven configuration.

Tying the Double-Loop Figure Eight

1. Take a bight of rope and cross it back over itself, forming a loop.

2. Take two strands of the bight and wrap them around the standing part, then poke them through the loop.

3. To finish, take the loop at the very end of the bight and fold it down and around the entire knot you've just formed.

The double-loop figure eight is a great knot to use to equalize two gear placements. You can manipulate the knot by loosening one strand and feeding it through the body of the knot, shortening one loop, which makes the other loop larger. Unlike the double-loop bowline, the double-loop figure eight does not require a backup knot.

Double-Loop Bowline
(aka Bowline on a Bight)

This is another great knot for pre-equalizing two anchor points. It's very handy for clipping into a 2-bolt anchor. Back it up with half a double fisherman's knot if the tail end is near the body of the knot, as it can shift a bit when weighted.

Tying the Double-Loop Bowline

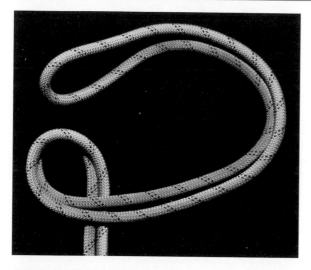

1. Take a bight of rope and cross it over the standing part.

2. Thread the bight through the loop you've just formed.

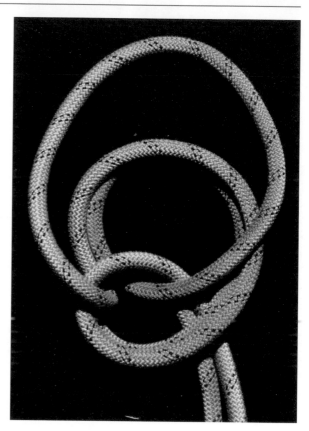

3. Configure the end of the bight in a loop above the rest of the knot.

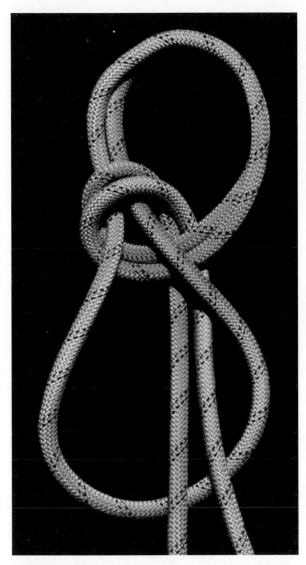

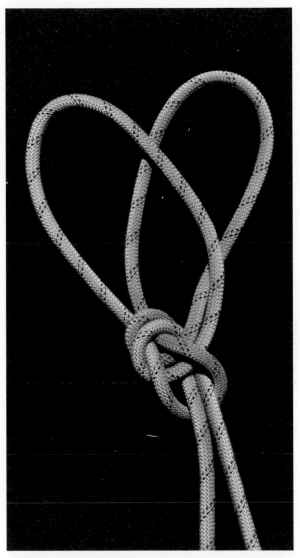

4. Flip the loop down like a hinge behind the rest of the knot.

5. Pull on the two loops until the end of the bight tightens at the base of the knot.

The two loops can be adjusted by feeding one strand into the body of the knot, which alternately shortens one loop and lengthens the other.

Knots for Webbing

Nylon webbing is a slick material that should be tied with caution. There have been many accidents where poorly tied knots in nylon webbing have failed. The two recommended knots for tying nylon webbing into a loop are the water knot (also known as the ring bend) and the double fisherman's knot (also known as the grapevine knot). When you tie the water knot, your finished tails should be a

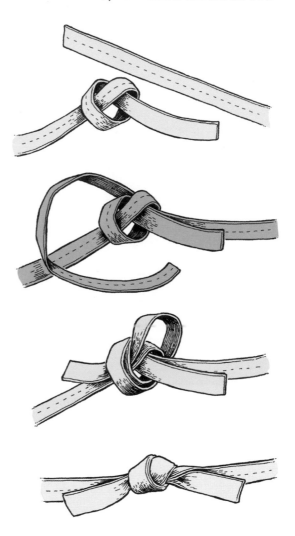

Tying the water knot (ring bend)

minimum of 3 inches in length. It is important to tighten the water knot properly, as it has a tendency to loosen if tied slackly in a sling that is being used over time.

Why would you even use nylon webbing tied with a knot as opposed to a sewn runner? A sewn nylon runner is stronger than the same material tied with a knot. The answer is for rappel anchors when you tie slings around a tree or through bolt hangers. It is also sometimes useful to untie the knot, thread it through something (like a tunnel), and retie it.

The double fisherman's knot is also a good knot to use to tie nylon webbing into a loop, although it does require more length of material to tie and is very difficult to untie after it has been seriously weighted.

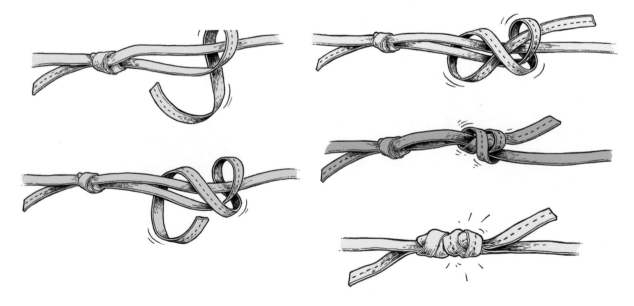

Tying nylon webbing with a double fisherman's (grapevine) knot

Bends

A bend is a knot that joins two ropes or lengths of cord together. These knots are used to tie your cordelette into a loop and also to tie two ropes together for toproping or rappelling.

Figure Eight Bend

A variation of the figure eight follow-through, this knot can be used to tie two ropes together. It has superior strength and is easy to untie after it has been weighted. It is simply a retraced figure eight. On 9mm- to 11mm-diameter rope, tie it with the tails a minimum of 5 inches long.

The figure eight bend

Double Fisherman's Knot for Cord and Rope

This is the preferred knot for joining nylon cord into a loop to make a cordelette. It is also a very secure knot to tie two ropes together for a double-rope rappel, but it can be difficult to untie.

The double fisherman's knot

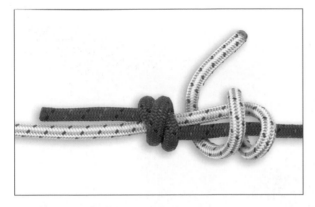

Tying the double fisherman's knot (aka grapevine knot). When tying 7mm nylon cord, leave the tails about 3 inches long.

Triple Fisherman's Knot

For 5mm- and 6mm-diameter high-tech cord (i.e., with Spectra, Dyneema, or Technora core), a triple fisherman's knot tests slightly stronger than the double fisherman's.

To tie a triple fisherman's knot, make three wraps before feeding the cord back through.

The triple fisherman's knot

Knots for Joining Two Ropes

Standard knots for joining two ropes include the double fisherman's knot and the figure eight bend. The double fisherman's is more difficult to untie than the figure eight bend once weighted; the figure eight bend, while relatively easy to untie, is bulky. Tie these knots with a minimum of 3 inches of tail, and carefully tighten the knots before using them. A stiff rope makes it harder to cinch the knots tight, so be especially careful with a stiffer rope.

Which knot you use should be based on several variables. If the ropes differ drastically in diameter, or are very stiff, the most foolproof knot is the figure eight bend, backed up with half a double fisherman's knot on each side. This is a bulky knot, but it gives you a real sense of absolute security.

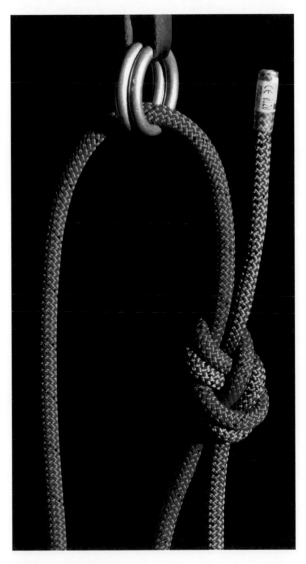

Figure eight bend

Figure eight bend with fisherman's backups

Flat Overhand (aka Euro Death Knot)

How this knot received the "Euro Death Knot" moniker is unclear. Most likely the knot was initially adopted by Europeans and deemed unsafe when first seen by American climbers unfamiliar with its use. As far as I know, it has been responsible for only one rappelling accident in recent times (in the Tetons, September 1997), when it was sloppily tied with too short a tail. Ironically, in July of that year, former *Rock and Ice* magazine editor George Bracksieck had written that "the one-sided overhand knot (tails parallel and together) remains the best knot for rappelling. . . . Be sure to leave plenty of tail and to set it snugly."

After analyzing the accident, Grand Teton ranger Mark Magnusun wrote: "I intend to do some additional research in an effort to gain information on the overhand knot used for joining ropes, the origin of the 'Euro-death' nickname, and incidents of other failures."

From 1999 to 2009 various tests revealed the flat overhand knot to be roughly 30 percent weaker than the double fisherman's for tying two ropes together, but still plenty strong for rappelling situations. Testing also revealed that it was virtually impossible to get the knot to fail—as long as it was tied with a suitable-length tail and properly tightened.

Flat overhand knot

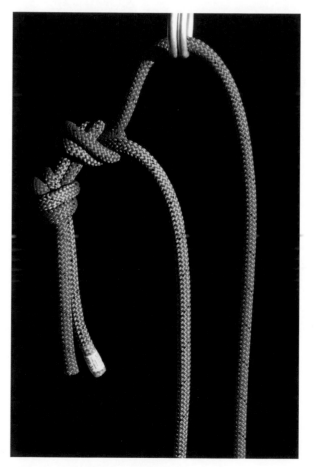

Flat overhand with overhand backup

Petzl, a leading manufacturer of rappelling devices, recommends using the flat overhand for joining two rappel ropes together, if the ropes are of similar diameter and the tail is a minimum of 20cm (8 inches).

The flat overhand has become widely adopted as *the* knot for joining two rappel ropes of similar diameters because it is easy to tie and easy to untie after it has been weighted, and it presents a clean profile when pulled down the cliff as the ropes are retrieved, thus less likely to jam in a crack. Multi-pitch guides often tie their cordelettes with a flat overhand so that the knot can be easily untied and the cordelette used for other applications. For added security it can be easily backed up simply by tying another flat overhand right on top of the first one, although this adds bulk.

There are a few cautions, however: The flat overhead knot is not recommended for tying together two ropes of drastically differing diameters (e.g., 7mm to 11mm), or for use on very stiff ropes. The bottom line is that the knot should be used with discretion, well tightened (pull as hard as you can on all four strands), and tied with a long tail (minimum of 8 inches). Personally, I use the flat overhand (with a second overhand backup) in situations where I'm concerned about the knot possibly jamming in a crack when I pull the rope down for retrieval. Otherwise I use a figure eight bend or double fisherman's.

The flat overhand is a very poor choice for use with nylon webbing, and it has been responsible for numerous rappel anchor failures where it was tied in webbing with a very short tail. An even worse knot for rope and webbing, and a knot responsible for numerous accidents, is the flat figure eight, which inverts at shockingly low loads as the knot rolls inward and capsizes. The flat eight is a knot to be avoided and is very dangerous if tied with short tails, especially in nylon webbing.

Hitches

A hitch is a knot that is tied around something. The clove hitch is used to fasten a rope to a carabiner. A friction hitch is a knot tied with a cord or sling around another rope, utilizing friction to make the knot hold when it is weighted, but releasable and movable without untying when it is unweighted.

Clove Hitch

The clove hitch is tied around the wide base of a carabiner. The beauty of the clove hitch is easy rope-length adjustment without unclipping from

Tying the clove hitch

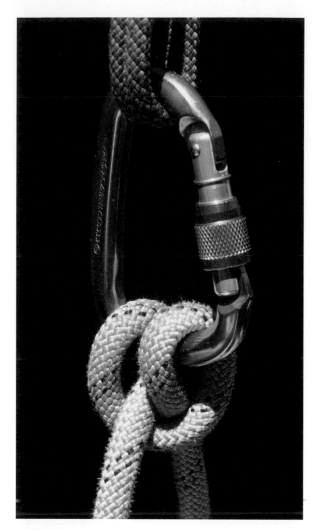

Finished clove hitch

Prusik Knot

A prusik knot is used for rope ascending and as a component in many rescue systems. It can be loaded in either direction. To tie a prusik, first make a "prusik cord" out of a 3-foot, 9-inch length of 5mm- or 6mm-diameter nylon cord tied into a loop with a double fisherman's knot. The 3-foot, 9-inch length also works well for the autoblock knot. Buy the softest, most pliable nylon cord you can find, because a softer cord will grip best. To tie the prusik, simply make a girth-hitch around the rope with your cord, then pass the loop of cord back through the original girth-hitch two or three more times. Dress the knot to make sure all the

A four-wrap prusik

the carabiner, making it a truly versatile knot for anchoring purposes: for anchoring a belayer, tying off an anchoring extension rope, or tying off the arms of a cordelette.

Get in the habit of tying the load-bearing strand on the spine side of the carabiner, and you'll ensure that you're loading the carabiner in the strongest configuration. Make sure you tighten the clove hitch properly by cranking down on both strands, and you're good to go.

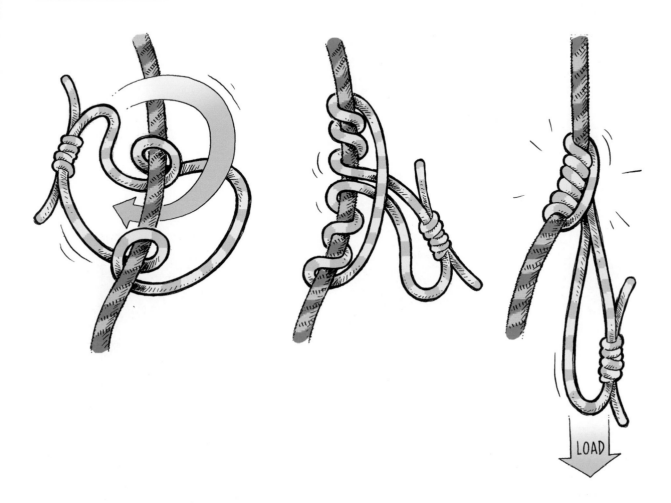

LOAD

strands are even and not twisted—a sloppy friction hitch will not grip as well. Test the knot before using it. A thinner cord will grip better, but below 5mm in diameter the cord will be too weak for many rescue applications. To slide the prusik after it has been weighted, loosen the "tongue," which is the one strand opposite all the wraps.

Tests on various friction hitches reveal that the prusik consistently has the most holding power in a wide array of cord and rope combinations, so use the prusik in scenarios (like 3:1 raising systems) where it will be loaded with more than body weight.

Klemheist Knot

This is another useful friction hitch that is quick and easy to tie, and it's a good choice as a rope-ascending knot, especially if you're forced to use a sling rather than a piece of cord to tie a friction hitch. If using a sling, pick a nylon one over a Dyneema sling, because it grips better and is less susceptible to weakening if it gets hot (nylon has a higher melting point). Four wraps of 6mm cord or 18mm (¹¹⁄₁₆-inch) width sling tied on a single 10mm-diameter rope usually work well. After the hitch has been weighted, loosen the tongue (the one strand opposite all the wraps) to slide it more easily.

Tying the Klemheist Knot

*Completed klemheist knot
tied with cord*

Autoblock

Sometimes called the "third hand," the autoblock is used to back up your brake hand when lowering someone, or to back up your brake hand when rappelling. Tie it with your loop of 5mm- or 6mm-diameter nylon cord wrapped three or four times around the climbing rope. When I tie it on a single strand of 10mm-diameter climbing rope (as in a lowering situation), I usually make four wraps. For a rappel backup on a doubled 10mm rope, I usually go with three wraps.

The autoblock with nylon cord. To construct an autoblock, I've found that a good length of cord is 3-feet, 9-inches, tied with a double fisherman's knot. Select the most pliable 5mm or 6mm nylon cord you can find.

The Sterling Hollow Block, shown here wrapped in an autoblock configuration, is a 100 percent Technora sling designed specifically for use with friction hitches.

Munter Hitch

Tied on a carabiner, the Munter hitch can be used for belaying, lowering, and rappelling. It can be tied off and released under tension, a benefit that makes it a key knot for rescue and assistance applications. The Munter can be tied off and secured with a mule knot.

Tying a Munter Hitch

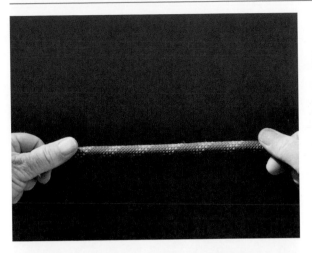

1. Grasp a single strand of rope with both hands, with thumbs pointing toward each other.

2. Cross the right-hand strand on top of the left-hand strand; hold the two strands where they cross with your left thumb and forefinger, then slide your right hand down about 6 inches.

3. Now bring the right strand up and behind the loop.

4. Clip a locking carabiner where the forefinger is shown here, below the top two strands.

Mule Knot

The mule knot is a hitch that can be used to secure a Munter hitch or tie off a tube-style belay device. The Munter/mule/overhand combination is an ugly looking knot, but the beauty of the mule knot is that it is releasable under tension, which makes it a key knot for many rescue applications.

Tying a Mule Knot

1. When tying a mule knot, be aware that when the rope is under tension (holding a climber's weight), you'll need to keep a firm grip on the brake strand.

2. Keeping the load and brake strands parallel, form a loop on the brake strand by crossing it behind while still maintaining your grip with your brake hand.

3. With your non-brake hand, take a bight of rope and pass it through the loop you've created with the load strand in between the loop and the bight. Snug the mule knot up tight against the Munter hitch.

4. Pull some slack, and finish with an over-hand loop backup.

Tying Off a Tube Device on the Spine of a Carabiner

1. Pass a bight of rope through the carabiner and form a loop. If the device is under tension, pinching the rope against the device with the opposite hand will help lock it off.

2. Pass a bight of rope through the loop you've created, with the spine between the loop and the bight.

3. Finish with an overhand loop backup on the load strand in front of the device.

Stopper Knot

This knot is used as a safety knot in the end of a rope. It is essentially half a double fisherman's knot tied on one strand of rope. A stopper knot prevents the end of a belay rope from passing through the belay device, and prevents rappelling off the end of the rope if rappelling with a tube device (e.g., ATC) or assisted braking device (e.g., Grigri). When using two ropes, I tie a separate knot at the end of each rope, as tying both ropes together can cause the ropes to twist around each other.

Tying a Stopper Knot

It sounds almost too simple, but the best way to avoid rappelling off the end of your rope is simply to tie a stopper knot in the rope's end. The stopper knot can, however, pass through a figure eight descending ring, so if you're rappelling with that particular device and want a safety knot at the end of your rope, you'll need to use a bulkier knot that cannot pass through the device.

Finished stopper knot. Make sure the knot is cinched tight to prevent unravelling.

CHAPTER 8

Belaying and Lowering

Belaying involves three major elements: managing the slack in the rope, maintaining a brake hand on the brake strand of the rope, and stopping the fall. Belaying is a big responsibility; if you take on the task, you should be competent and alert, and you should know the proper safety checks and belay signals.

Manual Braking Devices

The most commonly used belay/rappel device is a manual braking device (MBD), essentially a tube or slot device (with two slots so it can be used for both belaying and rappelling on a doubled rope). When the two strands of rope (one going to the climber, one to the belayer's brake hand) are held parallel, in front of the belay device, there is little friction; but when the brake strand is held at a 180-degree angle relative to the strand going to the climber, the device affords maximum friction, making it relatively easy to hold the force of a falling climber.

Learning the proper hand movements is key to becoming a safe belayer. There are many techniques acceptable for a safe belay with an MBD, and they all have this in common: They effectively manage the slack, while still maintaining a brake hand on the brake strand side of the rope, and they generate enough friction to stop a fall and safely lower a climber.

Over the last decade, advances in technology have allowed manufacturers to produce thinner ropes, and belay devices have evolved along with

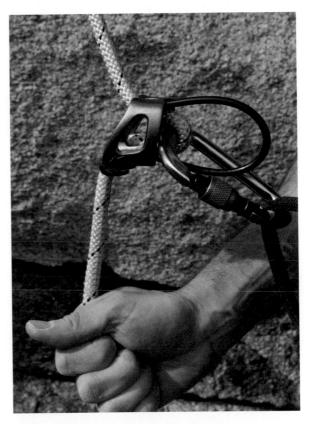

Black Diamond ATC XP belay device

Toproping Space Odyssey (5.10a), Joshua Tree National Park, California

the ropes. When buying a belay device, check the manufacturer's specifications and make sure it's appropriate for the diameter of your climbing rope. The most popular MBD is the Black Diamond ATC (tongue in cheek for "air traffic controller"), which also comes in a more versatile version with teeth on one side (the ATC XP) that gives the belayer two options: a regular friction mode when the brake strand is on the non-teeth side, and roughly twice the amount of friction when the brake strand is on the teeth side.

Multipurpose Devices: Autoblocking Devices

Several manufacturers make hybrid tube devices (e.g., the Black Diamond ATC Guide and the Petzl Reverso) that have both a manual braking mode and an autoblocking or "assisted braking" mode, making them versatile choices that can be used for both belaying and rappelling in the regular manual mode, or for belaying directly off the anchor in the autoblocking mode. The main disadvantage to these multipurpose devices is the difficulty in lowering a climber when the rope is under tension.

Black Diamond ATC Guide in "guide," or autoblocking, mode

Petzl Reverso in autoblocking mode

Assisted Braking Devices

Assisted braking devices (ABDs) with self-locking cams have become popular for sport climbing. The most popular ABD is the Petzl Grigri. These devices are designed to lock when suddenly weighted, as during a fall, but might not lock under certain circumstances—for example, if there is a slow and accelerating pull, when the handle is pressed against the rock or carabiner, when the belayer grabs the rope on the non-brake hand side, or when the belayer grabs the device incorrectly and holds the cam down, preventing it from locking. For these reasons it is important to remember that, even

though ABDs are self-locking, a brake hand should always be maintained on the brake side of the rope. These devices are far from foolproof, and many accidents have occurred with ABDs, typically when someone is being lowered, the handle is pulled all the way open, and the belayer loses control of the brake hand. The Petzl Grigri Plus is a new design that addresses this problem with a built-in anti-panic function that essentially locks the device when the handle is opened too far when lowering.

Petzl explains some of the advantages of the Grigri Plus: "The design of the handled camming mechanism enables exceptional descent control. The selector knob allows you to choose between two belay modes: toprope or lead climbing. The toprope mode and anti-panic handle make the Grigri Plus particularly suitable for learning how to belay."

As with any belay device, the cardinal rule to remember is this: Always maintain a brake hand!

If for some reason you need to take your brake hand off the rope, tie a backup knot (e.g., overhand loop) on the brake strand side of the rope.

ABDs are very useful for direct belays. Their main advantage over multipurpose devices is that they allow an easy lower when the rope is under tension. When lowering with a direct belay using an ABD, the brake strand should be redirected. I'd recommend using gloves when belaying with ABDs, since they'll allow you to put more weight on your brake hand for smooth lowers.

Petzl Grigri in lowering mode

Seek proper instruction from a certified guide or experienced climber if you have any doubts about how to use the device or the proper technique to use when belaying with the device.

Someone's life is, literally, in your hands; and if you're the belayer, it's your responsibility to know what you're doing.

Standard Climbing Signals

Proper use of the universal climbing signals, along with a methodical safety check, are integral parts of a safe climb. Ambiguity in the use of climbing signals has led to many tragic accidents, simply because of lack of communication between the climber and belayer. One infamous tragedy occurred in a toprope setup at a popular ice climbing area when the climber reached the top of the climb (at the top of the cliff) and the anchor. The climber yelled, "I'm OK!" but the belayer thought he heard "Off belay." The belayer unclipped the rope from the belay device and took the climber off belay, thinking he was going to walk off the top. The climber leaned back to be lowered and fell to his death.

On a yo-yo toprope climb, it's important to be vigilant at the transition from the climb up to the lower down. This is where most accidents due to improper communication and climbing signals occur. There should be no ambiguity. If I'm the climber, I always hold onto the strand of rope that goes back down to my belayer until I am sure he or she has heard my command and is in the brake position and ready to hold my weight. In most cases you'll be within visual contact, so in addition to hearing the verbal commands, you'll want to look down over your shoulder and visually verify that the belayer is being attentive, with his or her hand in the proper brake position, alert and ready to lower you safely. In situations where you are climbing with other parties around you, it's best to include your partner's name in the signal (e.g., "Off belay, Bob.") to prevent confusion, although I once saw a leader who was in the middle of a pitch on a crowded multi-pitch crag get taken off belay when someone else yelled "Off belay, John," and there was more than one John. So be vigilant and be heads up.

Here are the standardized climbing signals I've used for more than thirty-five years in my climbing school:

On belay? Climber to belayer, "Am I on belay?"

Belay on: Belayer to climber, "The belay is on."

Climbing: Climber to belayer, "I'm beginning the climb."

Climb on: Belayer to climber, "Go ahead and start climbing; I have you on belay."

Up rope: Climber to belayer, "There is too much slack in my rope. Take up some of the slack." (Too much slack in the belay rope will mean a longer fall. Remember that rope stretch also contributes to the total distance of a fall, especially when there is a lot of rope out in a toprope scenario.)

Slack: Climber to belayer, "Give me some slack; the rope is too tight."

Tension (or Take): Climber to belayer, "Take all the slack out of the rope and pull it tight; I am going to hang all my body weight on the rope." (This could be a situation where the climber simply wants to rest by hanging in the harness while weighting the rope, or a toprope situation where the climber is getting ready to be lowered back down a climb.)

Tension on (or **I've got you**): Belayer to climber, "I've taken the rope tight, and my brake hand is now locked off in the brake position, ready to hold all your weight."

Lower me: Climber to belayer, "I'm in the lowering position (feet wide, good stance, sitting in the harness, weighting the rope, and leaning back), and I'm ready to be lowered."

Lowering: Belayer to climber, "I'm proceeding to lower you."

Off belay: Climber to belayer, "I'm safe. You can unclip the rope from your belay device and take me off belay." (Never take someone off belay unless you hear this signal. The universal contract between belayer and climber is that the belayer must never take the climber off belay unless the climber gives the belayer the "off belay" command.)

Belay off: Belayer to climber, "I've unclipped the rope from my belay device and have taken you off belay."

That's me! Climber to belayer, "You've taken up all the slack in the rope, and the rope is now tight to my harness."

Watch me! Climber to belayer, "Heads up! Be attentive with the belay—there is a good chance I'm going to fall right here!"

Falling! Climber to belayer, "I'm actually falling; go to your brake position and lock off the rope to catch my fall!" (A fall can happen so fast that the climber might not be able to shout this signal during a short fall, but it helps the belayer react more quickly, especially in situations where the belayer can't see the climber.)

ROCK! Climber to belayer and others below, "I've dislodged a rock and it's now free-falling below me—watch out below!" (The equivalent signal to "Fore!" in golf, "ROCK!" should also be yelled when the climber drops a piece of equipment.)

Belaying from the Base

The best way to belay from the base of a climb in a toprope situation is to attach the rope and belay device directly to the belay loop on your harness with a locking carabiner. The rope then runs through the top anchor and back down to the climber. Your body weight serves as part of the anchor, and the added friction at the toprope anchor makes it relatively easy to catch a fall, hold a climber who is hanging on the rope, or lower a climber back down. The belay device is right in front of you and easy to manipulate. In situations where the climber far outweighs the belayer, or when the belayer is precariously perched on uneven terrain, the belayer should have a ground anchor. *A direct belay (directly off the anchor) is not recommended for toprope belaying from the base.*

Chris Baumann is one of California's most experienced rock climbing instructors. He offers these fine points on how to set up a manual belay device (like an ATC) when belaying from the base:

When setting up your locking carabiner and ATC or similar device, a righthanded belayer should place the carabiner on the belay loop with the large end facing outward and the spine of the carbiner on the right (gate pointed left).

If your belay device has high and low friction options, pick now by placing the teeth downward for more friction or up for

Belayer with a good stance, braced against the cliff to resist an upward pull.
PHOTO BY CHRIS BAUMANN

less friction. Push your rope through the right-side slot of the device (spine side) with the climber's end of the rope going up and the brake strand of the rope going down.

Chris teaches the fine points of belaying technique and stresses the importance of a good stance:

I find it far less physical to keep my belay motions small, trying not to reach as high as I can with my left hand when I pull down, keeping my elbow bent when I pull in rope. You will end up doing the BUS motion more times but it takes less energy.

1. The BUS (brake under slide) method of belaying on a toprope. Start by clipping the rope into the slot in the belay device closest to the spine side of the carabiner and orient the rope so that the brake side is down.

2. To take up rope, pull the rope up with your brake hand (palm down) as you simultaneously pull the rope down with the other hand . . .

3. . . . then brake the rope down under your belay device.

4. Take your non-brake hand and firmly grasp the rope directly under the belay device . . .

5. . . . then slide your brake hand up against that hand and repeat the process. This technique is easy to learn and maintains a firm brake position on the rope at all times. In a fall, remember that the brake position is down.

Many people have neck pain when they belay. Try standing at a 45-degree angle and looking up over your shoulder. If you are right-handed, position your left side forward with your right foot to the back. Your neck will appreciate it, and the angle makes for a much stronger and safer belay stance.

Along with body positioning, the stance is important. It's ideal to have your front foot very close to or up against the wall. This will keep you from being dragged across the ground if the climber falls or the weight increases dramatically when lowering the climber. By raising your foot up and pushing against the wall at a 45-degree angle, you can hold and lower a larger person much easier and more securely.

It's OK to stand away from the cliff only if the climber and belayer are close in weight and the ground the belayer is standing on is flat or slopes uphill toward the climb. When the ground slopes upward from the base of the cliff, or when there is a chasm between the belay stance and the cliff, the belayer can be pulled off their feet—violently swinging and slamming into the rock. This is when you want a ground anchor.

After you've mastered the BUS method, a more advanced technique is to brake under and switch the brake hand, alternating back and forth with either hand. As a professional guide, in a day's belaying I can pull more than 1,000 feet of rope, which can really work your shoulders, especially if there's rope drag. I prefer this method, as I can alternate arms/shoulders rather than tiring out one arm/ shoulder.

The Ground Anchor

The worst accident I've had in forty years of rock climbing happened when I was belaying in a toprope situation without a ground anchor. I was belaying from the base of the climb in a relaxed position about 15 feet out from the base of the cliff. Between the ledge I was belaying from and the cliff itself was a deep chimney. My partner was climbing on a toprope and suddenly fell while attempting an overhang about 50 feet above me. He swung wildly in the air. I easily caught the fall and locked off my belay device in the brake position, but I was pulled off my stance, swinging 15 feet straight into the wall like a pendulum. I braced for the impact with an outstretched leg and sustained a severely

sprained ankle. A simple ground anchor would have prevented this accident. Belaying accidents are common, and in almost every case they have the same element: no ground anchor.

In a toprope situation, if both the climber and belayer are roughly the same body weight and the terrain at the base of the cliff is flat, a ground anchor is unnecessary. But if the climber far outweighs the belayer, a ground anchor should always be considered. If the climb is vertical or overhanging, more force will be exerted by the falling climber than a fall on a low-angle climb. It is especially important to establish a ground anchor for the belayer in uneven terrain, particularly if the belay stance is perched high on top of boulders, or is some distance away from the base of the cliff.

Two-Rope Toprope Setups

Wan rigging long topropes of more than half a single rope length, two ropes can be tied together using a double fisherman's knot or figure eight bend knot. With such a huge amount of rope out between the climber and the belayer, rope stretch is a major concern, especially if you are using dynamic ropes. Remember that even a short fall in a toprope situation will stretch a dynamic rope about 10 percent, so tighten up the rope when belaying someone just off the ground or just above a ledge.

There are two methods that can be used to deal with the knot joining the two ropes. The simple solution, also the best if there will be no stance for the climber to stop at, avoids the knot pass altogether. With the knot joining the two ropes at the anchor, tie a figure eight loop and attach it to the climber's belay loop with two locking carabiners (gates opposed and reversed). When the climber reaches the anchor, the knot will be just above the belayer's device, so no knot pass is required.

Another solution is to use two belay devices. The climber ties into the end of the rope as usual. The belayer anticipates the knot pass and has a second belay device clipped to his belay loop, at the ready. When the knot reaches the belayer, the belayer alerts the climber to find a good stance, then ties a backup knot (figure eight loop) on the brake hand side of the belay device. The belayer steps forward to create a bit of slack, then clips the rope into the second belay device on the climber's side of the knot, leaving the first belay device clipped in. If another person is available, he or she can assist the belayer simply by holding the rope with both hands under a little tension above the belay device as the belayer accomplishes this. When the climber reaches the anchor, the belayer lowers him until the knot is almost to the belay device, and the process is reversed: The climber takes a stance, the belayer unclips the second belay device (first double-checking that the first belay device is still clipped in and has the backup knot), then the belayer unties the backup knot and lowers the climber as normal.

Belayer ground anchored in uneven terrain. Remember ABC: The anchor, belayer, and climber's direction of pull should all come into a straight line. Her tie-in strand is on her brake hand side, so she won't spin awkwardly if the system is loaded. The clove hitch knot is recommended for this application, since it allows you to easily adjust the length of your tie-in based on your stance.

Belayer anchored to a ground anchor with a clove hitch. If the climber far outweighs you, a ground anchor is useful, even on flat ground. When you're lowering, come tight against the anchor to help brace yourself and bolster your stance.

A good system to rig a ground anchor is to start with the belayer tying into the end of the rope. Not only does this "close" the rope system, but it allows the belayer to use the climbing rope to connect to a ground anchor with a clove hitch, which can be easily adjusted to suit the stance.

Natural anchors are obvious choices for ground anchors, like a sling or cordelette around a tree or a large block of rock. A single bomber cam or nut in a crack will also suffice.

If you are the belayer in a toprope scenario, anticipate that you will be pulled in a line directly to the toprope anchor master point, and anchor and brace yourself accordingly. Ideally, the ground anchor will be low and directly behind or beneath you or just slightly to the side. Remember your ABCs: anchor, belayer, climber. There should be a straight line between the anchor, the belayer, and the direction of pull created by the climber.

Belaying from the Top

When belaying from the top of the cliff, the belayer can choose from a variety of belay methods, depending on the situation. Since it's a given that you'll have the climbing rope to work with, if you're belaying from the top, the simplest and most efficient way to anchor yourself is to tie in to the climbing rope and connect yourself via the rope to the master point of your anchor with a clove hitch on a locking carabiner. This allows you to adjust the length of your rope connection depending on your stance. Ideally, you'll want to position yourself so that you can see your climber for the entirety of the climb, or the entirety of the lower if you're lowering someone down the cliff.

Belaying off the Harness: The Indirect Belay

Using the indirect belay method, the belayer clips the rope and belay device into a locking carabiner attached to the belay loop on her harness. The belayer is "in the system," which means that if the climber falls, the belayer's body will absorb the force of the fall to some extent. I call it "indirect," since the force generated in a fall does not necessarily go directly onto the anchor. For example, if the belayer takes a sitting stance and braces with her legs against a rock outcropping, and the climber falls, the belayer can absorb the force of the fall without transferring any load onto the anchor, accomplishing this by the stability of the stance aided by the

Belaying with an indirect belay. The belayer is in a good seated stance, with his rope clipped to the anchor's master point. The ATC XP belay device is attached to his belay loop. If the climber below falls, the belayer will have to absorb all the force and bear the full weight of the falling climber onto his harness. The braking position will be awkward, and since the belayer is slightly out of line from the direction of pull to the anchors, he will get pulled into that line. The belayer should simply position himself in line (anchor-belayer-climber, or ABC) to remedy this potential problem. My choice in this situation would be to belay with a direct belay, using my Grigri.

friction of the rope running over the surface of the rock and at the belay device itself. When using the indirect belay, the anchor and stance are important, because if the belayer gets pulled off balance, or pulled sideways, she can easily lose control of the belay. The belayer should anticipate the direction

1. The old-school "pinch and slide technique" is commonly used as an indirect belaying technique when belaying from the top of a cliff. Start with the brake hand (the right hand in these photos) next to the belay device, with the left hand extended.

2. Pull the rope in with the left hand and simultaneously pull rope out with the brake hand.

3. Move the brake hand back behind the braking plane (more than 90 degrees from the angle of the rope going to the climber) and pinch the rope above the brake hand with the left hand ...

4. ... then slide the brake hand down toward the belay device.

5. Move the left hand back to the extended position and repeat the process. The cardinal rule to remember with this method is to always keep the brake hand on the rope.

she will be pulled if a fall occurs and position herself accordingly, tight to the anchor. The ABC abbreviation works in this situation: The belayer should be in a line between the anchor and the climber (anchor-belayer-climber).

While the indirect belay is commonly used by most recreational climbers, it is rarely used by trained, professional guides—for a number of reasons. One is that the belayer is trapped "in the system," and if a climber falls, the climber's weight is hanging directly off the belay loop of the belayer, making it difficult for her to even move. Once in this position, it is awkward for the belayer to hold the fallen climber, particularly if the stance is bad. Lowering the climber from the top of the cliff using an indirect belay can be difficult, if not dangerous, particularly if the cliff is steep and the climber far outweighs the belayer.

The indirect belay is also the worst method to use if the belayer needs to provide any assistance (like a raising system) to the climber below, since the belayer is trapped in the system and would need to perform a "belay escape" in order to get out of the system and convert it to a raise.

If this sounds complicated, that's because it is! I detailed these steps to illustrate a point: An indirect belay is a poor choice for belaying a second. The only situation where I would consciously seek to use an indirect belay is when the anchor is marginal and I don't trust it. I'll still clove hitch my rope to the anchor's master point with a tight connection, but then I'll take the best stance I can and brace myself so that my stance, and the falling climber's weight on my harness, absorbs the force of the fall, not the anchor.

The Redirected Belay

This technique utilizes the additional friction generated by running the rope back through the anchor to help assist in catching a fall. Clip your belay device into your harness belay loop, then run the rope back through a locking carabiner at the anchor master point. If you're using a cordelette-style anchor setup, you can also redirect the rope through a locking carabiner clipped to the "shelf," which is defined as all the loops in the cordelette

Escaping the Belay

If you are belaying with the belay device clipped to your harness and need to escape from the system, follow these steps:

1. Tie off the belay device with a mule knot.

2. Tie a friction hitch (klemheist or prusik) on the load strand going to the climber.

3. Attach the friction hitch to a locking carabiner and tie a Munter/mule with the climbing rope (off the back side of the knot connecting you to the anchor).

4. Back up the system by tying the rope directly into your anchor, before releasing your mule knot at your belay device, to transfer the load onto the Munter/mule/friction hitch system.

The redirected belay. If the climber below falls, the force on the belayer will be directly in line to where the rope is redirected through the anchor. The friction of the rope running over the redirect carabiner will absorb some of the force.

just above the master point knot. If your partner falls, you'll be pulled toward the anchor, so brace yourself for a pull in that direction. Because of the rope's friction through the redirect carabiner, you have to hold only about two-thirds of the force generated in the fall. The redirect nearly doubles the force on the anchor (just like in a toprope rig), so if you decide to use a redirected belay, the anchor should be bomber. The drawback to this technique, like the indirect belay, is that if any rescue or assistance skills are required, it's more complicated to rig any raising system. If the climber far outweighs the belayer, in the event of a fall, the belayer can be pulled violently in toward the redirect, so if you're the belayer, brace yourself accordingly. One advantage of the redirected belay is that the extra friction makes it easy to smoothly lower the climber, especially with an ABD.

The Direct Belay

The method preferred by most professional guides when belaying a follower is the direct belay. In a direct belay the belay device is clipped directly to the anchor, and in the event of a fall, the anchor, not the belayer, bears the brunt of the fall and holds the climber's weight.

Using an MBD like an ATC *is not recommended for use in a direct belay*, because unless the device is positioned below your waist level, the braking position will be very awkward, and you will be in a weak and dangerous position to hold a fall. If the master point is above your waist level, the Munter hitch works well, since the braking position for maximum friction is when the two strands of rope are parallel to each other, with the brake position down below the carabiner, not above it.

The best way to set up a direct belay is to use an ABD like a Grigri, or an autoblocking device like the ATC Guide or Petzl Reverso, attached directly to the master point on the anchor. The advantage of a Grigri or similar device is that in the event of a fall, the Grigri simply locks off and the anchor

The direct belay. A Grigri is clipped directly to the master point. As long as the anchor is bomber, this is my preferred method. One caution: Beware of situations where, under load, the Grigri can come in contact with the rock, which can impede its braking function. Always maintain a brake hand.

holds the climber's weight. When using a Grigri in the direct belay mode, take care when the device is close to rock, as anything that presses against the handle (i.e., the rock) will release the locking mechanism. Be sure to position the handle away from the rock.

Remember, an MBD or similar non-autoblocking device is *not recommended* for use in a

Detail of a direct belay setup using a quad rig

Another method of rigging a quad for a direct belay

A direct belay with a Munter hitch. Here the belayer's right hand is her brake hand. The starting position (left photo, position 1) is with the brake hand at the top and the guide, or feel, hand at the bottom. Pull the rope down with the brake hand as the guide hand goes up. Feeding the rope up with the guide hand, rather than pulling the rope down tightly with the brake strand, puts fewer kinks in the rope. The brake hand stays on the rope as the guide hand grabs below it. Then return to position 1. Unlike a manual braking tube device, maximum friction with a Munter hitch is when the two rope strands are parallel.

direct belay if the master point is at or above the belayer's waist level, as the braking position would be very awkward.

Assistance from the Top

3:1 Raising System

One reason to use the direct belay technique with an ABD when belaying is that it is easily converted to a 3:1 raising system (aka the Z system) in a matter of seconds. As a climbing guide, my first choice is always providing the anchor is bomber, because it allows me to anticipate and prepare for any eventuality, like a quick lowering or raising of the climber. I use my Grigri, clipped directly to the master point or extended master point (using the climbing rope).

If you're direct belaying with an autoblocking device (e.g., Black Diamond ATC Guide or Petzl Reverso), the 3:1 system enumerated here will still work, but you'll have way more friction in the system, which will make the raise much more difficult.

To set up a 3:1 raise, follow these steps:

1. Tie a backup knot (overhand loop) on the brake strand side of the Grigri. Now you're "hands free" and can take your brake hand off the rope.
2. Tie a friction hitch (prusik or klemheist) on the load strand going down to the climber.
3. Clip the brake strand side of the rope (from the Grigri) to a locking carabiner clipped to the friction hitch. Now untie the backup knot and pull up on the brake strand side of the rope. Pulling 3 feet on your end raises the load 1 foot. Friction is your enemy when raising with a 3:1. If the rope going to the climber is in contact with a large surface area of rock, the raise will be correspondingly more difficult. A pulley at the friction hitch carabiner reduces friction and makes it easier to pull. Remember, this technique is for assisting a climber, helping him get past a tough

Also known as the Z system, the 3:1 raising system is easy to rig if you're already using a Grigri for a direct belay. The Grigri is the ratchet (which locks off when you need to reset), and the friction hitch (in this example, a klemheist knot) is your tractor (which moves up and down the field).

spot, not for hauling up a severely injured or unconscious climber.

4. When the friction hitch is all the way to the Grigri, reset the friction hitch by sliding it back down toward the climber. The Grigri's built-in ratchet will lock off and hold the load as you do this. Then continue the raise.

3:1 Assisted Raise from a Direct Belay

For this method the climber must be close enough that you can throw her a bight of rope. The climber clips the rope into her harness to assist in the raise. Using this system allows both the climber and rescuer to work together, and makes it much easier for the rescuer to raise the climber.

If you are the belayer/rescuer, the steps are as follows:

1. Tie a backup knot (overhand loop) on the brake strand side of your ABD (autoblocking device).
2. Toss a bight of rope down to the climber and have her clip it into her belay loop with a locking carabiner.
3. Identify which strand the climber should pull on by shaking it.
4. Untie the backup knot.
5. The climber pulls down as you pull up on the brake strand side of the rope. Warn the climber to watch her hands so they are not pinched in the carabiner as you pull.

A 3:1 assisted raise. With the climber also pulling, you get a tremendous mechanical advantage, making it far easier to raise someone than with an unassisted 3:1 raise.

The Rope Direct Belay

If the belay anchor is initially built well back from where you can see your follower, and you want to belay from a stance to maintain a visual on the person who's climbing up from below, you can use the climbing rope and a rope direct belay technique, which is essentially belaying off an extended master point. Clip your climbing rope to the master point

Another method of rope direct belay rigging useful for belaying from the top on a single-pitch climb. The belayer is on the right strand of rope, attached to the master point with a clove hitch to a locking carabiner. Off the back side of the clove hitch, the rope is clipped back to a separate carabiner with a figure eight loop. Off this strand, the Grigri is clipped to another figure eight loop. Here the distance is fairly close to the anchor, but this rigging technique is most useful for greater distances between the anchor and your desired belay stance, limited only by the length of available rope. The big advantage is visual contact with your climber in situations where the anchor is some distance back from the edge.

Guides often use this rope direct method in single-pitch situations where the anchor is well away from the edge and they want to position themselves to better watch their clients, and perhaps lower them back down when they reach this point. It is essentially an extended master point, created by running the lead rope through carabiners at the anchor's master point (I prefer two lockers, opposed and reversed), lowering down to the preferred position, then tying an overhand knot on both strands, creating another two-loop master point. While the loop extending up to the anchor is not redundant, it's monitored, and it's your full rope strength.

on the anchor with two locking carabiners (opposed and reversed), then lower yourself to your preferred stance (you can use an ATC or Grigri to accomplish this), then tie a BHK. The master point loops on the BHK should be within arm's length so that you can easily belay from these with an ABD. I call this method "rope direct" because you are essentially belaying directly off the anchor, albeit extended whatever distance is required to position you at the edge. Using a device like a Grigri, you'll have the benefit of a quick and easy conversion to a raising system if required, and it's easy to lower someone on this setup by redirecting the brake strand on the Grigri (see "Lowering").

Lowering

It's often easier and quicker to lower someone back down a single-pitch climb than to have her rappel. Depending on the belay device you're using, the lowering procedure can range from simple to relatively complicated, so have this in mind when considering which belay device will work best for a particular situation. Lowering with an indirect belay

is dangerous, especially if the climber being lowered far outweighs the belayer, particularly if there is a severe transition from a flat ledge to a vertical cliff.

Lowering with a Grigri

My first choice is always to lower someone using a Grigri. Since it has a built-in autolock, there is no need to back it up with an autoblock. Petzl sells the Freino, a carabiner that has a special gate on the side for the brake strand to be clipped into, to facilitate lowering. Without the special carabiner, you can redirect the brake strand back up through a separate carabiner clipped to the master point (or, on a cordelette anchor, up to the shelf). The big advantage of the Grigri is that once the rope is clipped in,

A Grigri in the lowering mode with the brake strand redirected using the Petzl Freino carabiner, which is specifically designed for this application.

A Grigri rigged for lowering with the brake strand redirected through a carabiner clipped to the master point.

you can use it for lowering (just remember to redirect the brake strand!) or belaying (as the climber climbs back up), and it's all set to rig a 3:1 hauling system if your climber needs some assistance on the way back up.

Lowering with a Munter Hitch

Flake the rope at your feet so that if there are any tangles, you can get to them. If you're anchored with a clove hitch, it's adjustable, so you can fine-tune the length of your tie-in as required. If the stance at the anchor allows you to see down the cliff and watch the climber as you lower him, clip another locking carabiner (a large, pear-shaped carabiner works best) to the master point and tie a Munter hitch. Back it up with an autoblock clipped to a locking carabiner at your belay loop, and you're ready to lower your climber.

MULE KNOT

The mule knot is used to tie off a Munter hitch. The great advantage of the Munter-mule combination is that it can be tied off and released when the rope is weighted and under tension, making it one of the key knot combinations for many rescue applications.

The belayer is ready to lower the climber with a Munter hitch on a locking carabiner clipped to the master point, backed up with an autoblock clipped to a locking carabiner attached to the belayer's belay loop.

Lowering with a Munter hitch and an autoblock. The belayer is holding an autoblock backup that's clipped with a locking carabiner to his belay loop.

Using an Autoblock Knot as a Backup When Lowering

Whenever you are lowering a climber with a manual braking device, it's best to back up your brake hand with an autoblock knot clipped to a locking carabiner attached to your belay loop.

Some guides call the autoblock the "third hand," because if you take your brake hand off the rope when you're lowering or rappelling, the autoblock grabs the brake strand of your rope like your hand would. The autoblock adds an extra level of safety, especially when there are tangles in your rope that you need to untangle as you lower your climber or descend on a rappel.

In a single-pitch setting, if the stance at the anchor does not allow you to see down the cliff and watch the climber as you lower him, you can rig the rope direct belay system to position yourself at the edge to maintain visual contact. As a guide, I always strive for visual contact with my clients whenever belaying or lowering them.

Lowering with a Redirected Manual Braking Device

To lower a climber with an MBD like an ATC, you can clip the ATC to your harness and redirect the climber's strand back through the anchor at the master point. This adds friction and makes it easier to hold the climber's weight but increases the load on the anchor—in fact, it nearly doubles it. Also, if the climber far outweighs the belayer, it can be very awkward and difficult to lower the climber, because the belayer is getting pulled into the anchor.

Another technique is to clip the ATC directly to the anchor master point and redirect the brake strand back through a locking carabiner at the master point (or, on a cordelette anchor, the shelf, which is all the loops in the cordelette just above the master point knot), to maintain the proper angle (for maximum friction) on the brake strand. Back it up with an autoblock attached to your belay loop with a locking carabiner. If you're using a manual

A manual braking device (Black Diamond ATC XP) rigged with a redirect for lowering. The climber's end is coming out of the left side of the belay device, and the brake strand is redirected up through a carabiner clipped to the shelf.

braking device like an ATC or similar tube device, remember, *do not use an MBD for a direct belay* if the device is at your waist level or above, as the braking position would be weak, awkward, and dangerous.

Lowering with an Autoblocking Device

If you're using an autoblocking device (like the ATC Guide or Petzl Reverso) and belaying a second with a direct belay in the autoblocking mode, if the second falls, the device locks off. Lowering from a locked device under tension presents a challenge, and there are a variety of solutions based on the situation.

For very short lowers (inches), or to provide slack, you can simply grab the blocking carabiner firmly and ratchet it up and down. Make sure you have a firm grip with your brake hand on the brake strand.

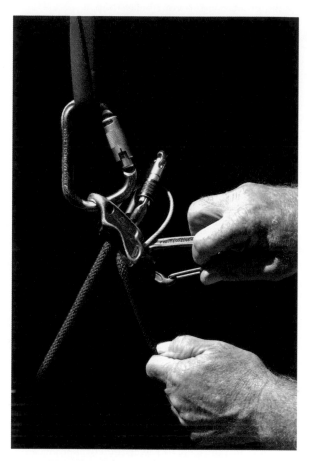

For a short lower (a few feet), you can use a small carabiner (it's a good idea to have one dedicated in advance for this application) clipped to a small hole in the autoblocking device. Pulling up on the carabiner releases the autoblocking function. Autoblocking devices can be unpredictable, and can release suddenly, so an autoblock backup is recommended. Tie the autoblock knot on the brake hand strand, and clip it to your harness belay loop with a locking carabiner.

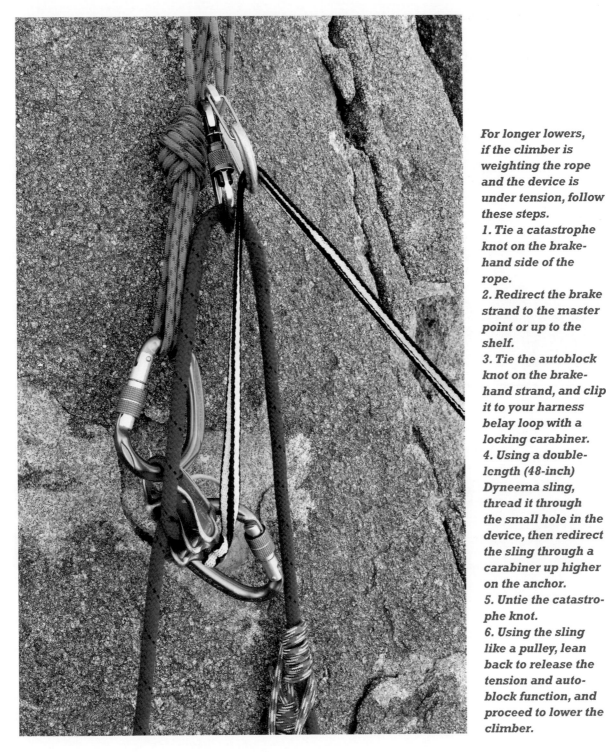

For longer lowers, if the climber is weighting the rope and the device is under tension, follow these steps.

1. Tie a catastrophe knot on the brake-hand side of the rope.

2. Redirect the brake strand to the master point or up to the shelf.

3. Tie the autoblock knot on the brake-hand strand, and clip it to your harness belay loop with a locking carabiner.

4. Using a double-length (48-inch) Dyneema sling, thread it through the small hole in the device, then redirect the sling through a carabiner up higher on the anchor.

5. Untie the catastrophe knot.

6. Using the sling like a pulley, lean back to release the tension and autoblock function, and proceed to lower the climber.

If you are using a direct belay with an autoblocking device and the plan is for your second to be lowered once he or she reaches your stance, you can easily convert the autoblocking device to the manual breaking device mode once the climber reaches the ledge or stance and is ready to be lowered.

1. Redirect the brake strand, then tie an autoblock knot on the brake strand and attach it to your harness belay loop with a locking carabiner.

2. Clip another locking carabiner to the master point, and clip in the autoblocking locking carabiner on the device (carabiner to carabiner; check that both are locked).

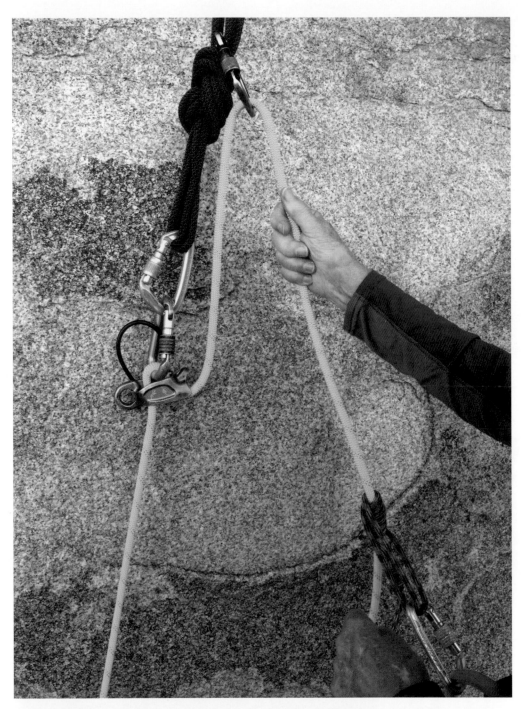

3. Now you're ready for a smooth lower in the manual braking mode, brake strand redirected and backed up with an autoblock knot.

Terri Condon rappels at the Buttermilks, Bishop, California.

PHOTO BY BOB GAINES

Rappelling

The descent from the top of a toproping crag usually entails a walk-off trail or a Class 3 descent off the side or back of the cliff, but in most situations, once you've set up a toprope anchor and want to begin climbing, it will be most expedient to rappel straight down to the base. Making the transition safely from the top of the cliff to a rappel is more complicated when you have a toprope setup rigged with an extension rope, since you have to reach the climbing rope below the edge. Doing this safely is detailed in chapter 6 (the Joshua Tree System).

Many cliffs also have fixed anchors for rappelling. These are typically trees (often a single, bomb-proof tree with slings and rappel rings) or, more commonly, a 2-bolt anchor rigged with metal rings through which you can thread your rope. If the rappel anchor is in an exposed location near or at the edge of the cliff, you'll want to safeguard yourself by clipping in to the anchor with a personal tether, like a sling or PAS while you rig the rappel.

Your rappel anchor should be redundant. Even if it's just a single, big pine tree, inspect the slings and rings for redundancy. The rigging should have two separate slings around the tree and two rings through which you can thread your rope.

To rappel with an ATC or similar tube device, thread a bight of both strands of rope through the device and clip them in to a locking carabiner attached to your belay loop. Keep the cable on the ATC clipped in to the carabiner while you do this so that you won't drop the device. As you thread

A well-engineered rappel anchor with all stainless steel hardware. Most modern rappel anchors will have a combination of chain, quick links, and rings, and should exhibit redundancy.

Proper rappelling stance for good stability, with a slightly crouched position and wide base for the feet, looking over one shoulder to watch where she's going

I placed this rappel anchor at the top of a popular cliff at Joshua Tree National Park. All the components are stainless steel and painted before installation to match the color of the rock.

Tree rappel anchor with two slings and two rings

Black Diamond ATC XP rigged for a double-rope rappel in high-friction mode

the ropes through your device, position the brake strands down, toward your feet. This will allow the rope to feed smoothly through the device with no twists. If you have a device with different friction options, like the ATC XP, decide if you want more or less friction. (With the ATC XP, placing the teeth side down on the braking side will give you the most friction; non-teeth side down, less friction.) How much friction you want depends on these variables: the diameter of the rope, the slickness of the rope's sheath, your body weight, and the angle of the rock face you're rappelling down.

For a steep rappel I prefer to hold the ropes with both hands below the device in the braking position, with the ropes going down between my legs. For less-steep rappels, I hold the ropes off to my right side, since I'm right-handed, and grab the ropes with my right hand as my brake hand at my hip.

Rappelling Safeguards

Tethering

To rig a rappel you'll want to protect yourself if you're at the cliff edge, or if you've climbed up on a toprope and want to transition from toproping to rappelling. Always protect yourself by tethering to the anchor with a sling or daisy chain, like the Metolius PAS (personal anchor system) or Sterling Chain Reactor. I prefer the Sterling Chain Reactor, since it's made of nylon rather than Dyneema so that it has a bit of stretch. Likewise, if I'm tethering with a sling, my choice is to use an $\frac{11}{16}$-inch double-length (48-inch) nylon sling over a Dyneema sling. No matter what material you use for a tether, be careful not to climb above the anchor, since if you slip you'll experience a mini factor 2 fall (total distance of the fall divided by the length of your attachment), which creates a high-impact force and may result in a wrenched back or bruised ribs.

Know the difference between a traditional daisy chain with bartacked pockets and one constructed loop to loop. It's a little confusing, since manufacturers refer to both designs as "daisy chains."

A traditional daisy chain with bartacked pockets (not loop-to-loop construction) is not recommended as a personal tether or for rappel extensions, because clipping a carabiner into two loops is a very weak and dangerous connection (3 kN/674 lb.).

The PAS (personal anchor system) style construction is a chain-link-style loop-to-loop construction, without the weakness of bartacked pockets.

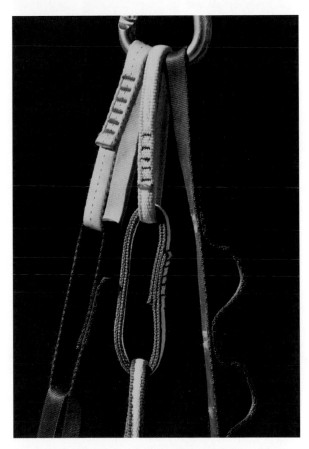

Tether comparison: Left to right: Sterling Chain Reactor with loop-to-loop construction, Metolius PAS with loop-to-loop construction, Black Diamond Daisy Chain with traditional bartacked pocket construction

No! A traditional daisy chain with bartacked pockets like the one shown here is not recommended for rappel extensions or as a personal tether, because if you clip a carabiner into two loops, you create an extremely weak and dangerous connection (3 kN/674 lb.).

Metolius manufactures several PAS designs made from a Dyneema-nylon blend, including their PAS 22 (rated at 22 kN/4,950 lb.) and their Ultimate Daisy Chain, which they say is "the only daisy chain to pass the CE/UIAA sling standard, the Ultimate Daisy has a strength of 22 kN (4,950 lb.) in any configuration, thereby eliminating the potential dangers of traditional daisy construction."

The Sterling Chain Reactor is rated at a minimum breaking strength of 2,810 pounds when girth-hitched to a harness. According to Sterling Ropes, the Chain Reactor "is a multi-functional daisy chain designed with full-strength loops frequently used for personal connections and extending rappel devices. Made from our nylon webbing, each individual loop is full strength and can withstand and absorb forces."

Preventing Rappel Accidents

Although rappelling is a simple technique, statistically a high percentage of rappelling accidents end in a fatality. Why is this? Perhaps rappelling is so rudimentary that the fine points of safety are sometimes overlooked. Analyzing rappelling accidents tells us what can go wrong. Let's take a look at two scenarios in some detail.

SCENARIO 1: RAPPELLING OFF ONE OR BOTH ENDS OF THE ROPE

Believe it or not, this happens with some regularity, and almost every year there are several fatal rappelling accidents in America where someone has simply rappelled off the ends of a rope. It also happens when the ends are uneven on a doubled rope rappel. When the short end passes through the rappelling device, only one strand of the doubled rope remains in the device, and the climber's body weight will rapidly pull the rope through the rappel anchor, quickly dispatching the climber to the ground. A simple solution is to tie knots separately in both ends of the rope using stopper knots. It's a key safety habit in the single-pitch environment, no matter what you're using the rope for.

SCENARIO 2: NOT CLIPPING BOTH STRANDS OF THE ROPE INTO THE CARABINER

This is an easy mistake to make if you're not alert and double-checking your system. If you thread both strands of rope through your rappel device, but clip only one strand into your locking carabiner, when you lean back and weight the rope, you'll descend as rapidly as in the first scenario, and with equally injurious or fatal results. A good safety habit is to first clip in with a sling to the rappel anchor, rig your rappel device, then weight the rappel system and double-check everything *before* unclipping the sling. Always go through a mental checklist before rappelling: ABCDE. "A" is the rappel anchor. Take a look at the anchor, slings, chains, etc., and make sure the rappel rope is threaded properly through the anchor. The anchor should be redundant all the way to the point where your rope is threaded through the anchor. What this means is that you should not rely on a single piece of gear in your anchor system, whether it is a single cord, sling, or rappel ring. "B" is for buckles on your

harness—double-check to make sure they are buckled properly and doubled back appropriately. "C" is for carabiner. Make sure the locking carabiner that attaches your rappel device to your harness is being loaded properly on the long axis—and check to make sure that it is locked! "D" is for down—look down to confirm the rope is long enough to reach the destination. "E" is for ends of the rope—make sure you have stopper knots tied in the ends, so you don't rappel off one or both ends.

Rappel Belays

If you're teaching a beginner who is rappelling for the first time, it's best to belay him or her on a separate rope. Another technique to back up somebody on rappel is called the fireman's belay. This is done

Fireman's belay

by having someone down below attentively holding both strands of the rappel rope (in a doubled rope rappel). When this person pulls down on the ropes and applies tension, the rappeller will stop on a dime—he or she cannot move down the rope when it is under tension.

Rappel Backups

In the old days, the most common method for a rappel backup was using a prusik knot on the ropes *above* the rappel device, connected to the harness with a sling. The non-brake hand would cup the prusik knot and hold it in a loosened position during the rappel, allowing it to slide down the rope. Letting go of the knot allowed it to slide up and

grab onto the ropes, stopping the rappel. There are two drawbacks with this method. One is that for the prusik to lock off, it must hold all the rappeller's weight. The second is that once it is weighted, the rappeller must remove all his body weight from the prusik knot in order for it to be released, not an easy task if you're on a free-hanging rappel. In essence, to take your weight off the prusik, you might need the skills to perform a mini self-rescue.

The modern rappel backup utilizes the autoblock knot, rigged *below* the rappel device. There are two distinct advantages with this method. One is that for the autoblock knot to grab, it only needs to hold a very small percentage of the rappeller's

Black Diamond ATC XP rigged for rappelling with a three-wrap autoblock backup clipped to the leg loop with a locking carabiner

Extended rappel device with autoblock backup

weight, since it is on the braking side of the device, and the device itself is holding most of the weight and providing most of the friction. It is essentially like your brake hand squeezing and gripping the rope, and for that reason some instructors refer to it as the "third hand," like an angel grabbing your rope and averting a catastrophe, if for some reason you've lost control of the brake. The second big advantage of the autoblock method is that it is releasable under tension (i.e., when you've weighted it and it's grabbing onto the rope). As you rappel down, you simply take your thumb and forefinger, forming a circle (like the "OK" sign), and push the autoblock down as you go, allowing the rope to freely slide through the knot. When you let go, the autoblock knot rides up and grabs onto the rope, like your brake hand squeezing the rope. To release

In a pinch, the Munter hitch can be used for rappelling, although it will put some kinks in your rope. Position the gate of the carabiner opposite the braking side of the Munter hitch so there is no chance the movement of the rope can unscrew or open the gate.

Rappelling Safety Checks

Once the rappel ropes are set and threaded through the anchor, do an **ABCDE** safety check.

A. Check the **anchor** to make sure the rope is properly threaded, and that the anchor rigging is redundant.

B. Check the **buckles** on your harness.

C. Check the **carabiner** on your rappel device to make sure it's locked and that both bights of rope are clipped into the carabiner.

D. Look **down** and check the ropes to make sure they're not tangled and are long enough to reach the next anchor or the ground.

E. Tie stopper knots in the **ends** of the rope. If using a figure eight descender, tie both ends together with a BHK, and make sure the knot will be bulky enough to jam in the device.

the autoblock, even with your weight on it, is as simple as sliding it back down and holding it in the "open" position with your fingers. It's a beautiful thing and easy to rig.

The disadvantage of clipping the autoblock to your leg loop is that if for some reason you were to go unconscious and flip upside down, the autoblock could ride up and come in contact with

Here the PAS (a Sterling Chain Reactor) was clipped to the anchor for a tether while the rappel rope was threaded through the rings. The rappel device was extended and clipped into a loop of the PAS with a locking carabiner. An autoblock backup was clipped to the harness belay loop with a locking carabiner. Before unclipping the PAS, go through the ABCDE checklist and weight the system. If everything is A-OK, unclip the PAS from the anchor and you're good to go.

your rappel device, which would prevent it from grabbing, much like sliding it down and keeping it "open" with your fingers. In recent years professional guides have developed a method to safeguard against this, simply by extending the rappel device with a sling attached to the harness and rigging the autoblock clipped into the belay loop. I like to rig

a double-length sewn nylon sling threaded through both points at the front of my harness (where the rope tie-in goes through) and tied with an overhand knot, to gain redundancy at the sling. I prefer a fat nylon sling over a thin Dyneema sling for this application because nylon has a higher melting point. If the rappel rope is running across the sling,

A good way to tether yourself to a 2-bolt anchor is to use a PAS in conjunction with a quickdraw.

it could potentially create some heat due to the friction, which could damage the sling and reduce its breaking strength in later applications.

Rope Management

Tossing the Rope

There is an art to tossing a rope. The key is preparation—taking a little time for rope management will save you time in the long run. Several methods work well. One is to flake about half the rope (coming from the anchor) right at your feet, then butterfly coil the bottom half. Before you toss the rope, check that no climbers are directly below so that you don't toss the rope right on top of them. Make sure there are no loose rocks where you've flaked your rope, as the rope will launch any loose stones. If there are people directly below, yell "Rope!" and give them enough time to move out of the way before you toss it down. If there are trees at the cliff base, be careful not to throw the rope too far outward and get it hung up in a tree.

"Rope!" is the universal signal to use before tossing down a rappel rope. To prevent tangles, butterfly coil the rope first. At crowded climbing sites, when people are down below, a better method is to simply lower the rope from the ends until the entire rope is down.

Transition from Toproping to Rappelling

If you're toproping a climb and want to de-rig the toprope rigging and rappel off a fixed anchor (e.g., a 2-bolt anchor), the first thing you want to do is go over a game plan with your belayer. Numerous accidents have occurred due to miscommunications and ambiguities regarding what will take place at the anchor. As a belayer, never take your climber off belay unless you've been given the definitive "off belay" signal from your climber.

Transition from Toproping to Rappelling

Step 1: Attach yourself to the anchor's master point with a personal tether and a locking cara-biner. Call "Off belay" to your belayer.

Step 2. Pull up about 10 feet of rope, tie a figure eight on a bight (or overhand loop), and attach it to your harness with a carabiner.

Step 3. Untie your figure eight follow-through tie-in knot, and thread the rope end through the anchor.

Step 4. Tie a stopper knot in the end of the rope.

Step 5. Unclip the rope from your carabiner, and pull enough rope through the anchor to complete your rappel. If you're not able to see the end of the rope go all the way down to the ground (or get verification from your partner that the end is down), go to the middle mark of the rope. If you don't have a middle mark or bi-pattern rope, you can always measure from both ends to find the middle. My preference has always been to climb on bi-pattern ropes so that it's easy to find the middle. If you can't see it, check with your partner to see what's going on with the other end of the rope. Are they still tied in? Or is there a stopper knot?

Step 6. Rig your rappel device on your personal tether, and back it up with an autoblock attached to your harness belay loop with a locking carabiner.

Retrieving the Rope

One of the best days of climbing in my entire life was nearly ruined by a careless retrieval of a rappel rope. My exuberance changed to grave concern in the time it takes a tear to flow down a cheek. I had just rappelled to the ground after completing one of the most difficult free climbs I'd ever done,

Step 7. Clean the toprope rigging and you're ready to rappel.

in Eldorado Canyon, Colorado. I pulled my rappel rope to retrieve it, and just as the end of the rope passed through the rappel anchor rings, I called "Rope!" to alert my wife and partner, Yvonne, that the rope was coming down. She looked up, and the end of the rope, now whipping down with the sound of a fast jump rope slicing through the air, hit her squarely in the eye, temporarily blinding her. Luckily it wasn't a serious eye injury, but it could have been much worse.

I learned an important lesson that day—after that near-miss, I've always been more vigilant whenever I pull a rope down. First I make an assessment on where the rope will go; if anyone is in the path, I explain that I'm going to pull a rope and ask the person to move out of the way beforehand.

If it's windy, note the wind direction and where it will take the rope. Calling out "Rope!" as the rope comes sailing down is too late for anyone to move out of the way.

Before you begin pulling the rope down, look up and make sure there are no twists in it. If it's a long rappel, it's important for the last person down to safeguard against any twists and to be careful to separate the strands when unclipping the rappel device. If two ropes are tied together, make sure everyone in the party is clear on which rope to pull before you head down (e.g., "pull red"). If there is any chance of rope drag hampering the pull, do a test pull when the first person rappels down to ensure the rope can be pulled without jamming, and make any necessary adjustments (e.g., a longer sling extended over an edge) before the last person comes down.

There is a technique to pulling a rappel rope down, and it takes a little practice to get a feel for it. First double-check that there are no knots, kinks, or twists in the end you'll be pulling up toward the anchor. As the end approaches the anchor, slow your pull so that you can feel when the weight of the rope coming down toward you starts to pull the free end of the rope up toward the anchor without your assistance. Wait a second—for the end to pass through the anchor—then make an instantaneous sharp, forceful outward tug on the rope, which should fall away from the rock. Beware that a pulled rope can knock rocks off the cliff face, so be alert for rockfall. If all goes well, the rope will be lying in a big pile on the ground.

Teaching Rock Climbing in a Toprope Environment

If you're a recreational climber you may at some point want to take some of your friends climbing, or perhaps teach your children when they're old enough. If you do this, you've essentially taken on the role of instructor and responsibility for their safety.

The effective instructor is not someone who simply demonstrates a wealth of knowledge and expertise. It is someone who conveys information about what he or she knows in a way that others can readily comprehend, understand, and remember.

People have differing learning styles. If they're presented with an abstract concept (like a knot) and are not getting it, rather than being a question of intelligence, it's more likely that the way the information was presented does not suit their particular learning style. Often, taking a different approach with the presentation of the information will help in comprehension and retention.

Learning Styles

The three main learning styles I've encountered as an instructor are visual, auditory (verbal), and kinesthetic. Although most of us are some combination of different learning styles, we are usually predominate in one.

Visual learners pick up information most effectively by reading the written word and viewing photos or illustrations. They need to see it to learn it. This group represents the highest percentage of the population (roughly 65 percent), and they learn most effectively from written communication. Visual learners think in pictures and words. They prefer their information presented in a written format as opposed to the spoken word and usually prefer to take detailed notes when presented with verbal information. They can have difficulty with spoken directions. For example, a verbal description of how to get to some place is likely ineffective to them, but a written description along with a map would prove useful. For this group, charts, diagrams, graphs, and visual schematics are highly effective. When teaching a knot to this group, a verbal description is of little help; presenting the sequence of tying the knot like a schematic diagram, with step 1, step 2, and so forth, may prove more successful.

Auditory, or verbal, learners represent another large segment of the population (around 30 percent) and learn most effectively from the spoken word. They need to hear it to learn it. This group is composed of the most sophisticated speakers, and they relate most effectively to spoken words. They

Jose Maestas learning to climb at Ripple Wall, Red Rock Canyon Open Space, Colorado
PHOTO BY STEWART GREEN

are good listeners. They will listen attentively to a verbal presentation and take notes afterward. They benefit from lectures and participating in group discussions. They prefer their information presented in a verbal format, and for them information is not tangible unless it is spoken. They can have difficulty with written directions.

Another, much smaller percentage of people are kinesthetic learners, who learn by doing, by getting the feel and tactile sensation of performing the steps required to learn a task. They usually are gifted athletes and can learn a knot just by seeing it tied, then tying it themselves once or twice. I've worked with a number of the most elite US Navy SEALs (SEAL Team 6), and they are mostly kinesthetic learners, able to pick up abstract concepts like tying a knot very quickly. Kinesthetic learners prefer hands-on learning, but can appear slow if information is not presented to them in a style that suits their learning method.

Many people learn most effectively by watching, doing, and reflecting on a particular technique. Around 450 BC the great Chinese philosopher Confucius said: "Tell me and I will forget; show me and I may remember; involve me and I will understand." Various research studies point to the fact that

Learning knots at Joshua Tree National Park, California

people remember best by watching a demonstration, having a discussion, practicing the skill, then teaching it to others. Military trainers use the EDIP principle (explain, demonstrate, imitate, practice).

When teaching climbing techniques, I always try to present the topic in a way that most broadly targets all the differing learning styles. My approach is simple:

1. **Tell**
2. **Show**
3. **Do**

Using this approach, here is an example of how I would teach an abstract concept, such as a complicated knot:

1. **Tell.** A verbal explanation targets the verbal or auditory learning style, so I verbally describe the steps to tie the knot.
2. **Show.** I demonstrate the knot. Facing in the same direction (the mirror image) as the person you're teaching is helpful. This targets the visual learning style.
3. **Do.** I have the person I'm teaching practice tying the knot. This benefits the kinesthetic learner.

This is the basic approach, although there are additional teaching methods that will help in memory retention and learning, namely imagery and mnemonic devices. An example of using imagery when teaching the bowline knot: "The snake comes up through the hole, around the tree, and back down through the hole." Attaching a verbal image of an animal or thing is one of the most effective ways to remember an abstract concept. I've found this approach very effective for teaching the figure eight follow-through to large groups of 10-year-old Boy Scouts: "Make a face with the rope. OK, if this is the face, then where is the neck? OK, this is the neck, and this is the face. Take the rope and choke it behind the neck, then poke it into the face."

Mnemonic devices are another form of memory aid. The most common are abbreviations and acronyms. The military uses many abbreviations, like IED (improvised explosive device), SOTG (Special Operations Training Group), etc. In teaching climbing, we use abbreviations like ABC (anchor, belayer, climber), and acronyms like BARCK (buckle, anchor, rope, carabiner, knot), and RENE (Redundancy, Equalization, and No Extension).

To teach climbing techniques most effectively, take an approach that presents the information in a broad range of learning styles, then try to identify a person's particular learning style so you can aim directly at his or her individual style. If someone is not getting the information, change your approach and present it another way. Use imagery and mnemonics to help your students remember key principles (like safety checks or anchoring fundamentals), and chances are they will retain these key concepts throughout their climbing lifetime.

Learning from Mistakes

In my career as a rock climbing instructor, I've received training and undergone testing and evaluation of my guiding skills. The toughest lessons, but the most memorable ones, came from the mistakes I made that were critiqued by my mentors and peers. I've also found, in my role as an examiner for the AMGA Single Pitch Instructor exam, that candidates learn more and remember best from their mistakes when it really counts—when they're being scored in a pass-or-fail test situation. The harshest lessons in life are the ones we don't soon forget.

With students who have some experience under their belt, asking them to perform a task can tell you where to begin as an instructor. For example, one quick test I give new clients is to simply hand them the end of the rope with the instructions: "Go ahead and tie into the rope." How they accomplish this easy task tells me more about where they're at than even a brief interview.

One method I've used over the years when teaching anchoring fundamentals to a group class in a ground-school setting is to present a concept with a verbal presentation, a demonstration, and then a hands-on practice (tell-show-do). I give each student a scenario (e.g., this is the edge, here are the crack systems you can work with, build your anchor system so that your master point is here), then I let the students build an anchor system to their satisfaction, without constant coaching by me along every step in the process. By letting them finish without my input, they are likely to make some mistakes. Then, as a group, we go around and critique each anchor system setup. In this way everyone learns from everyone's mistakes. The big plus is that it gives me a valuable and instant diagnostic assessment of whether the students have grasped the concepts I've just presented and shows me what they (or we) need to work on to achieve our objective (e.g., a SRENE principle anchor system).

I also use this methodology when teaching a private lesson to one or two students who have a modicum of anchoring experience but have asked for a refresher course. I start by giving them a specific scenario, like rigging a toprope anchor, and let them rig it without any coaching. What I see in the final product of their anchor system helps me decide if they need to start with more basic concepts or can simply move on and build from a solid foundation to more advanced topics. I can then mentally prepare a lesson plan specifically targeted at their skill level and build upon their current foundation to reach our objective for the day.

Teachable Moments

A less formal way to present information is to explain and describe the technique as it comes up during the course of the outing or class. These are what I call teachable moments. For example, when setting up a climbing situation for novices, you can explain to them as they are tying in to the rope the importance of closing the system by tying a stopper knot in the other end of the rope. If they are on a slab climb and their heels come up and they tighten their leg muscles, explaining the correct technique of relaxing the calf muscles and dropping the heels is a teachable moment. Try to keep it positive. Many teachable moments occur when a simple mistake has been made, and addressing it at that very moment is a great way to teach someone the correct way to do something—the trick is to do it in a positive way that encourages the student to try something new and instantly improve or react positively to a potentially negative situation. Often, the ideal time to address a question is at the moment a particular event that illustrates a key point is occurring. This adds valuable context to the concept.

Taking Kids Climbing

Many kids are natural climbers with an instinctive curiosity and tendency to want to climb things. If you take kids to a rock climbing environment, they'll spontaneously want to explore, climb boulders, and scramble around on the rocks. The obvious danger, however, is that in a fall or slip they can get seriously scraped up, or worse.

Toproping is the safest method to use when taking kids climbing. Climbing develops muscular strength, balance, and kinesthetic awareness, and it introduces kids to valuable concepts like problem solving, teamwork, and the success that comes from perseverance and determination.

By age 8, 9, or 10, most kids will have reached the level of physical and emotional development to allow them to enjoyably experience climbing in a toprope setting. For younger children, the problem is not with the actual climbing but in having the balance and coordination to successfully be lowered down the climb, as this involves leaning back and weighting the harness, having control over the stance with the legs, and having the proper balance to control body position on the way down. Most very young children (under age 5) simply have not yet reached the level of physical coordination

Eight-year-old Galen Kozicki toproping at Joshua Tree National Park, California

Climbing involves teamwork, problem solving, and self-reliance. For young children, always use an adult backup belayer.

required to do this. But over the years I have seen precocious children with great balance (as young as age 3) who were physically talented enough to climb and be lowered down on a toprope.

Introducing kids to the climbing equipment before they climb helps instill confidence in the equipment. Give them a carabiner and explain how strong it is. Teach them a figure eight knot.

Show them how a belay device works. This will assuage their natural fears and help them trust the gear. Demonstrate proper use of their feet on edges and smears, and how to grab different handholds. Kids tend to look up as they climb, rather than look down and watch where they place their feet. Emphasizing that they look down and watch their foot all the way to placement on the hold will help.

Set up a short, easy climb on either a low-angle slab or a short wall with abundant hand- and footholds. Teach them the basic climbing signals. For their first time, have them climb up a short distance (say 10 feet above the ground), then go through the signals and have them lean back and weight the rope, get into the lowering position, and get lowered back down to the ground. This will show you if they possess the requisite balance to successfully be lowered down the climb. If they do, they are ready to climb a bit higher and repeat the same sequence. Take on a climb in small increments, and don't allow them to climb too high above the ground if they're not ready for it. You want the experience to be fun, not terrifying. If they're not yet able to be lowered down, they can swing around on the rope and play on the rock a little bit. There will be a next time. Just familiarizing them with the rope, harness, and equipment is a good start.

In recent years, kids' climbing equipment, including harnesses and helmets, has been introduced to the market. Wearing a helmet is important, since most young children have not yet developed a kinesthetic awareness of how to fall and stay in control, and are more likely to spin around and bump their head in the event of a fall. Consider a full body harness with straps over the shoulders for small children (under about 75 pounds) and very slender kids, as they lack prominent hip bones and could possibly slide out of a harness if they were to fall upside down. Shoes are one of the most important pieces of equipment for kids. I've seen many instances where a parent takes a kid climbing, demonstrates the climb (with climbing shoes), then puts the kid on the same climb wearing tennis shoes. This sets the child up for a lesson in frustration as his or her feet slide off every hold. Rock climbing shoes are the most important piece of equipment to instill confidence in children.

Teaching Climbing Movement

Just because you can run 100 meters in 9.7 seconds doesn't necessarily mean you'll be a great track and field coach, but it helps. If you have great talent and are able to effectively communicate, you have a winning combination. But I've seen many world-class climbers who were poor teachers, and many competent but not exceptional climbers who were excellent teachers. What I always look for in my climbing school are instructors who have both traits: talented climbers and patient teachers. Climbers who have mastered all the various climbing techniques at a high level can ultimately be the best teachers—their mechanics and fundamentals are so sound that they have the innate ability to easily demonstrate key concepts. But they also must be effective communicators and have enthusiasm, patience, empathy, and a desire to share their knowledge in a way that truly benefits their students.

When teaching technique, I try to present it in a way that most broadly targets the three learning styles: tell, show, and do. First I verbally explain the key elements of a particular technique and what to focus on. Then I demonstrate the technique, climbing the route and describing what I'm doing as I climb it. If I'm working with another instructor in a group class situation, I'll have the other instructor belay me while I climb and demonstrate so that the students can watch and listen without having to think about belaying. If I'm the only instructor, I'll have a student belay me, with another student as a backup belayer. If I have only one novice student with limited belaying skills, and I want to demo a climb to illustrate technique,

Instructor Lisa Rands demonstrates technique at Joshua Tree National Park, California.

I can either self-belay with an ABD or have the student belay me with an ABD. When I get to the anchor, I can either lower myself (by asking for some slack and clipping a rappel device or ABD on the single strand of rope that goes back down to my belayer) or simply clip into the anchor, go off belay, set up a rappel, and rappel down. If a student belayer is lowering me, before I lean back and let the belayer take my weight, I girth-hitch a sling to the belay loop of my harness and clip it into the single strand of rope running back down to my belayer with a carabiner so that the rope is within my grasp and I can maintain control if for some reason the belayer doesn't. If I want additional security, I can tie a prussik knot around the single strand of rope running down to my belayer and attach it to the belay loop on my harness with a sling and locking carabiner.

Before my students start a climb, I try to motivate them and, if necessary, allay their fears: "I know you can do it! Just try to stay as relaxed as you can, and remember, we've got you on a good belay."

I also give them a few specific things to focus on, but not so much that they are overwhelmed: "It's about using the least amount of strength, not the most." Or "Focus on your footwork; watch your foot go right to the hold. Be precise with your footwork. Climb with your eyes, and try to read the rock. When you get to a spot where you feel comfortable, stop for a minute and take a few deep breaths and relax. Remember—we'll keep you tight on the belay, so you can focus on doing the climb."

Once students are climbing, I give them verbal cues to maintain their focus: "Relax. Take a few deep breaths." Or "Keep your heels down." Keep your coaching positive, and encourage them with specific feedback that reinforces good technique: "Nice high step, I like the way you shifted your weight over the left foot." Or "Nice footwork, I like the way you are watching your feet all the way to the holds and placing your feet precisely."

After students finish their climb, I'll give them feedback that includes something specific to reinforce good technique: "Well done, nice footwork, you were really climbing with your eyes and picking out good footholds." Rather than criticize someone for what he or she did wrong, a better approach is to provide specific tips on what the person needs to do on the next climb to improve: "Try to relax your ankles and drop your heels down more."

Face climbing comes relatively naturally for most people. Many climbers have indoor climbing gym experience before they venture outside on real rock, so climbing a vertical face with positive holds is usually their forte, as it translates well to gym climbing. The subtleties of delicate friction and smearing are not something you can really learn in a gym, and crack climbing is a whole different animal. Many climbers with extensive gym experience can climb at a 5.11 level indoors, but they don't yet have the skills to jam a 5.8 crack. Crack climbing has a tougher learning curve, and it's important to put newcomers to crack climbing on routes that are easy enough to comfortably practice the various jamming skills. Taping their hands or having them wear crack gloves will give them more confidence to go for painful and possibly skin-ripping jams.

One technique we've used in my climbing school (developed by Erik Kramer-Webb) for advanced crack climbing seminars is to have the instructor on a fixed rope (jumaring with mechanical ascenders) alongside the student as the student is climbing and being belayed by another student on a toprope. The instructor can then give the student very specific coaching and demonstration, even putting a hand in the crack to show the best technique for a particular jam. This coaching method has proven very effective, and I've gotten great feedback from students when I've used it. With only one student, it is still possible to employ this technique: The instructor belays the toprope with an ABD attached to his belay loop, backing it up with a knot on the brake hand side if he wishes to stop and demonstrate a particular jam.

CHAPTER 11

Risk Management

Anatomy of an Accident

Proper risk management in the rock climbing environment involves identifying and assessing hazards and then making the right decisions to avoid them. If the hazards can't be completely avoided—climbing is not without hazards and risk—then controls to mitigate or minimize the risks should be implemented.

Every year the American Alpine Club publishes *Accidents in North American Mountaineering*, a comprehensive analysis of all the climbing accidents for the year. Studying what happened to other climbers can heighten your awareness of what to watch out for to avoid a mishap.

John Dill studied the most serious climbing accidents that happened in Yosemite Valley from 1970 to 1990. During that time fifty-one climbers died in accidents, 80 percent of those accidents, Dill estimates, "easily preventable." In his article "Staying Alive," Dill points out that state of mind is the key to safety: "It's impossible to know how many climbers were killed by haste or overconfidence, but many survivors will tell you that they somehow lost their good judgment long enough to get hurt. It's a complex subject and sometimes a touchy one. Nevertheless . . . at least three states of mind frequently contribute to accidents: ignorance, casualness, and distraction."

Ignorance is being unaware of a potential danger. Casualness is not taking things seriously enough—complacency reinforced by repeatedly getting away with practicing poor safety habits and having nothing go wrong. Distraction is when something takes your mind off the important task at hand, and your brain simply moves on to the next task without completely checking what you've just done.

My friend Kevin Donald, who used to run the International Alpine School in Eldorado Canyon, Colorado, had a business card he'd pass out to Hollywood producers when we worked together as mountain safety officers for film shoots. The slogan on his card: "Gravity Never Sleeps." I took that adage to heart, especially after a close friend busted nearly half the bones in his body and almost died after a 30-foot fall onto a concrete floor during a seemingly mundane rigging job for a commercial shoot in an airplane hangar.

Inattentional Blindness

"Inattentional blindness" is a term psychologists use to describe the neurological phenomenon that occurs when the brain fails to see something obvious when attention is distracted or focused on something else. Psychologists who study

Joshua Tree Search and Rescue Team in action at Joshua Tree National Park, California

multitasking have found that most of us aren't the multitaskers we think we are. Our brain is simply switching back and forth from one activity to another, deactivating one area of focus to process the other task. Think about it. When you make a mental error during the course of your day, it's almost always because you were thinking about something else, not the task at hand.

In my role as an examiner for guides' certification exams, I've seen examples of inattentional blindness many times during complicated technical scenarios, where the guide has moved his or her focus without seeing an obvious error, such as a carabiner unlocked at a key belay or rappel device. It's as though the mind skipped a step, or the brain said that everything was correct and complete when in fact it wasn't—a cognitive blind spot.

Psychologists theorize that once the brain determines what is important, it fills in the picture with whatever your expectations believe *should* be there. These failures of awareness happen to all of us at one time or another, but we're not aware of them, so we don't realize what we've missed! A systematic and routine checklist is helpful, but what we really need to look for is what might be wrong, not what looks right.

Don't be distracted when performing crucial tasks, and don't engage in conversation when tying in, clipping into anchors, rigging, making transitions, and performing technical scenarios. Get in the habit of double-checking your systems before engaging.

Pat Ament, the great Colorado climber of the 1960s and 1970s, writes in his book *Rock Wise*: "As with all of climbing, it is attitude that saves or kills. There is no better beginning than within the mind, in the form of complete concentration. There is no room for oversight or for dismissing what is logically understood. Keen intuition must evaluate all which strikes both mind and eye."

Rockfall

An example of an environmental hazard is rockfall, which can be naturally occurring (caused by melting ice, wind, etc.) or more likely human-made, caused either by someone pulling off or stepping on a loose hold or, in most cases, by a rope being pulled or dragged across the top edge of the cliff. Dropped equipment is also a hazard. As an instructor, at small crags I always establish a helmet perimeter zone at the base of the cliff—where inside the perimeter it's mandatory to wear a helmet—and require everyone to not hang out at the very base of the cliff in the rockfall zone unless they are belaying or climbing. An explanation of the risk is appropriate (i.e., why you need to wear your helmet at the base and while belaying and climbing), as is an explanation of the universal verbal signal for a falling rock or dropped piece of equipment: "ROCK!" Being vigilant is the best strategy, especially when other climbers are directly above or at the top of the cliff. Often what dislodges a rock is a rope being pulled around at the top of the cliff.

Terrain Hazards

Another environmental hazard is simply the terrain itself. If you're working on getting a group to the top of the cliff, simply falling off the edge is a hazard, as is any steep and exposed terrain involved in scrambling up to the top. In very exposed situations, a simple fixed line can be rigged, to which everyone can be attached using a sling and a prusik knot. Rig by girth-hitching the sling into the harness (through both points where the rope tie-in goes), then attaching it to a short loop of prusik cord with a locking carabiner. A nylon sling is preferable to a Dyneema one, since it has a modicum of stretch. Sliding the knot along the fixed line affords security and helps prevent anyone in your group from getting off-route onto a steeper or more exposed position.

Sign at US Marine Corps Mountain Warfare Training Center, Leavitt Meadows, California

The base of the cliff can also have terrain hazards. The ideal base for groups would be perfectly flat, but this is often not the case. Showing the proper approaches to the climb and belay spots and supervising them is important. Often the most dangerous aspect of taking a large group climbing in a toprope crag setting is their scrambling around on uneven terrain at the base of the cliff, unroped, where they aren't protected by a toprope. The use of ground anchors is important for the belayers in situations where there are chasms and drop-offs adjacent to the belay stances.

Closing the System

In both single- and multi-pitch environments, the rope system should always be closed. That should be your default. This simple protocol will prevent many accidents during lowering and rappelling. If a climber is rappelling and one rope end is too short, she can rappel off the short end, resulting in her pulling (rapidly!) the now free short end through the rappel anchor, quickly dispatching her to the ground. Another common accident occurs during lowering. If the belayer has wandered out a bit from the cliff, and the rope is too short and he's not paying attention to the end of the rope, the rope can travel through the belay device, resulting in a dropped climber.

A closed system means that both ends of the rope have a knot in them—either the end is tied into someone's harness or a stopper knot is tied on a free end. This simple safety habit prevents the end of the rope from ever going through a belay or rappel device. What I teach is *always close the system* unless there is a compelling reason not to do so. An example of a compelling reason? You know you're going to be pulling the end of the rope back up the cliff, since the knot can potentially jam in a crack as you're pulling it up the rock.

Safety Checks

If you haven't developed a safety check protocol, now is a good time to start. For me as an instructor, it's become second nature, and I'm a little shocked when I see recreational climbers who haven't developed the habit. I start with ABC: Check the ground anchor (if used), check the belayer, then check the climber. A proper safety check should be both visual and verbal.

Anchor

Check the ground anchor to make sure the belayer is in a line between the direction she will be pulled in the event of a fall and the anchor itself. A best way to attach the belayer to the ground anchor is with the rope, since it stretches, rather than a sling. The belayer is tied in, as normal, then clove hitches the rope to a locking carabiner attached to the ground anchor.

Belayer

Check the belayer's harness to make sure it is buckled properly. Check the figure eight follow-through knot to make sure it is (1) tied properly and (2) threaded through the correct tie-in points

at the front of the harness. Check the belayer's belay device to make sure the rope is properly threaded through the device. Lastly, check the belayer's locking carabiner on the belay device to make sure that it is locked. Check that the belayer is wearing her helmet.

Climber

Check the climber's harness to make sure it is buckled properly. Check the climber's figure eight follow-through knot to make sure it is (1) tied properly and (2) threaded through the correct tie-in points at the front of the harness. Check to ensure the climber is wearing his helmet.

These safety checks are simple, but you'd be surprised how many times I've caught students making a mistake somewhere along these lines. Do these checks before every climb. It's that simple.

One acronym to help you remember what to look for is **BARCK:**

B buckles on the harness
A anchor (check the ground anchor)
R rope
C carabiners locked
K knots

Whatever system you use, know what to check for, and be methodical with your safety checks.

Backup Belayers

The purpose of the backup belayer is simple: In case the primary belayer loses control of the brake, the backup belayer, holding the brake strand side of the rope, holds the rope to prevent a fall, essentially backing up the belayer's brake hand. For first-time belayers, it is appropriate for the instructor to be the backup belayer. For intermediate-level students who have demonstrated proficiency in belaying techniques, other students are commonly used for backup belayers. As an instructor, when you

Backup belayer in action

demonstrate a climb with a student belayer, adding another student as a backup belayer gives you an added layer of protection.

To properly back up a belay, the backup belayer should stand to the side of the belayer and simply hold the rope with both hands, taking in or feeding out rope as needed, leaving enough slack so that the rope is not being tugged from the belayer's brake hand or in any way impeding the belayer's ability to manage the belay. If the belayer loses control of the brake hand, the backup belayer essentially takes over the braking role. The critical juncture for the backup belayer is when the climber reaches the anchor and transitions into being lowered. The backup belayer can also help the belayer by managing the free end of the rope, preventing any tangles from reaching the belayer.

Experienced instructors often safely manage two climbs at the same time, engaging six participants simultaneously: two climbers, two belayers, and two backup belayers.

Another backup technique is the use of a "catastrophe knot." This is simply an overhand knot tied on the rope on the brake strand side of the belayer's belay device. As an instructor you can use the catastrophe knot if for some reason you need to walk away from your role as a backup belayer momentarily. If the climber falls and the belayer loses control, the overhand knot will jam in the belay device, preventing a catastrophic fall.

Falling

With a sound toprope anchor, a good belayer, a proper tie-in, and good safety checks, the biggest risks the climber faces during the climb are from falling. If the belayer is attentive, and there is minimal slack in the system, the fall will be short and uneventful. For novices, a demo on how to fall is important, showing them the proper position if a fall does occur: a wide stance with the legs, leaning back to weight the harness, not grabbing onto the

A discussion and demonstration on proper falling technique is appropriate for novices—feet wide, hanging in the harness, arms outstretched to brace against the rock, not grabbing the rope.

rope, extending both arms outward against the rock, not clutching the rock or grabbing handholds.

The falls to guard against and watch out for are falls when the climber is too far to the right or left in relationship to the toprope anchor, resulting in a swing or pendulum across the rock face, and falls when there is too much slack in the rope. Remember, if using a dynamic rope with a lot of rope in the system, rope stretch can be substantial (dynamic ropes stretch approximately 10 percent even in a toprope fall). When a climber is directly above the ground or a ledge, take particular care to ensure that the rope is slightly under tension (especially if you are using a dynamic rope) to guard against rope stretch in the event of a fall.

A directional can be used to prevent a swing in the event of a fall. A directional is a separate piece of gear placed below and to the right or left of the main anchor. For example, if the start of the route is 20 feet to the right of the toprope anchor, and the climber falls near the bottom, she will swing 20 feet to the left during the fall (or even hit the ground). A solid piece placed directly in line above the start would be a directional, preventing the swing. When the climber reaches the piece, she simply unclips and continues to the top. As the climber is being lowered, she re-clips into the directional so that the climb is ready for the next climber.

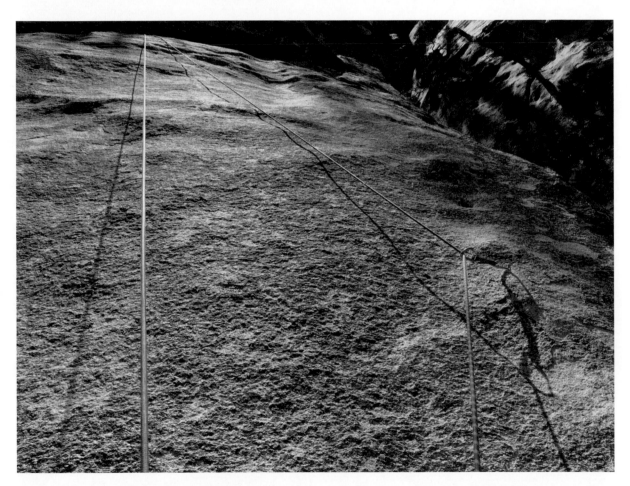

The right side of this toprope setup is clipped into a bolt that will act as a directional to prevent a falling climber from swinging.

Leave No Trace Ethics

You can practice Leave No Trace principles from the moment you step out of your car. The following simple steps will help keep the climbing sites we all share as clean as possible, with minimal degradation to the climbing area and the surrounding environment:

- At popular climbing areas, use the outhouses located at most parking areas before you embark on your approach to that day's chosen cliff.

- Always use marked climber's access trails where they are available. If there is no marked trail to the cliff, minimize your impact by walking on durable surfaces (e.g., a sandy wash, rock slab, or barren ground).

- At popular, easy-access crags, avoid making a beeline from the parking lot straight to the crag without first looking for an established path or trail. Walking off-trail can significantly impact vegetation and cause soil erosion if enough people do it over a period of time.

- If traveling in a group in more remote, pristine areas where no trail exists, fan out instead of walking in single file and try to walk on the most durable surfaces, avoiding fragile vegetation. Don't leave rock cairns to mark the path, as this takes away the challenge of route-finding from those who prefer to experience it on their own terms.

- If nature calls and you're far from any outhouse, deposit solid human waste well away from the base of any climbing site or wash by digging a cathole 4 to 6 inches deep. Cover and disguise the cathole when you're done. Pack out all toilet paper and tampons in a ziplock bag. Urinate on bare ground or rock, not plants. Urine contains salt, and animals will dig into plants to get at it.

- Leave no trace means just that—pack out everything you bring in, including all trash and food waste (that means apple cores and orange peels too). Set an example for your group by picking up any trash you find; plan ahead and always carry a trash bag with you when you go out to the crag.

- Don't monopolize popular routes by setting up a toprope and then leaving your rope hanging on the climb, unused. If your climb begins from a campsite, ask permission to climb from the campers if the site is occupied. Minimize your use of chalk, and if you're working a route, clean off any tic marks with a soft brush after you're done. Protect everyone's access to a climbing area by being courteous, beginning with parking only in designated areas and carpooling whenever

Patrick Paul belays Mike Roberts at The Needles, California.
PHOTO BY GREG EPPERSON

possible. Noise pollution can be a problem, from blasting tunes to yelling and screaming while attempting a hard climb. Be considerate and aware of those around you, and limit your noise production to a reasonable level.

- Pick up all food crumbs, and don't feed any wild critters—this habituates them to human food and encourages them to beg and scavenge, sometimes even chewing holes in backpacks to get at food. Consider leaving your dog at home—dogs dig and root up vegetation and stress native wildlife. If you do bring your dog, be sure to remove any dog poop from the base of the cliff and the approach trail.

- Leave all natural and cultural objects so that they can be experienced by everyone in their natural setting. If you are climbing in a national forest or national park, obey all regulations concerning the gathering of firewood and other objects.

For more information on Leave No Trace ethics, visit lnt.org.

Glossary

ABD (assisted braking device): A device that locks off the rope when a load is quickly applied. The most commonly used ABD is the Petzl Grigri.

aid: Means of getting up a climb using other than natural rock features such as handholds, footholds, and cracks, usually by hanging on the rope or equipment to rest and make progress up the climb.

aid climbing: Using equipment for direct assistance, which allows passage over rock otherwise impossible using free climbing techniques.

aid route: A route that can only be ascended using aid climbing techniques.

alcove: A cave-like formation or depression in the rock.

AMGA (American Mountain Guides Association): A national organization that trains and certifies professional climbing guides and instructors, promotes safety in guiding, and accredits guide services.

Aliens: Brand name for a type of spring-loaded camming device (SLCD).

American Triangle: A rigging method whereby a sling or cord is threaded through two anchor points and tied in such a manner as to create a triangular configuration that unnecessarily increases the forces on the anchor points. The larger the angle at the base of the triangle, the greater the force on the two anchor points.

arête: A narrow ridge or an outside edge or corner of rock.

arm bar: A technique for climbing an off-width crack by inserting an arm into the crack and utilizing counterpressure between the palm on one side of the crack against the triceps.

ATC (Air Traffic Controller): A belay/rappel device made by Black Diamond Equipment.

backpacker coil: A method of coiling a rope, also known as the "butterfly coil," that reduces kinking in the rope during coiling and facilitates carrying the rope like a backpack.

bartack: A high-strength stitch pattern used by climbing equipment manufacturers to sew slings and webbing into loops.

backstep: Placing the outside edge of the foot on a hold and turning the hip into the rock.

bail: To descend or retreat without successfully completing a climb.

bashie: A piece of malleable metal that has been hammered into a rock seam as an anchor; used in extreme aid climbing.

belay: Procedure of protecting a climber by the use of a rope.

belay device: A piece of equipment into which the rope is threaded/attached to provide friction for belaying or rappelling.

belayer: The person managing the rope on the end opposite the climber; responsible for holding the climber in the event of a fall.

belay loop: A sewn loop on the front of the climbing harness to which a rappel or belay device is attached with a locking carabiner; used when belaying and rappelling.

beta: Prior information about a climb, including sequence, rests, gear, clips, etc. "Running beta" is when someone instructs the climber on how to do the moves as he or she climbs.

beta flash: Leading a climb without falling or dogging, but with previous knowledge on how to do the crux moves, such as seeing someone else do the climb.

BHK: Short for "big honking knot," a double overhand on a bight forming two redundant loops; commonly used as a master point knot on a toprope setup using an extension rope.

bight: A bend in the rope where the two strands do not cross; used for knot tying, threading into a belay device, etc.

big wall: A long climb traditionally requiring at least one bivouac, but which may take just a few hours for ace climbers; *see wall.*

biner, biners: *See carabiner.*

bivi: *See bivouac.*

bivouac: To spend the night on a route, usually planned for on a big wall climb; also called "bivi."

bolt: An artificial anchor placed in a hole drilled for that purpose.

bomber: Absolutely fail-safe (as in a very solid anchor or big, big handhold); sometimes called "bombproof."

bombproof: *See bomber.*

bong: An almost extinct species of extra-wide pitons, which today mostly have been replaced by large chocks or camming devices.

bouldering: Short climbs on small boulders or cliffs performed without a belay rope, usually utilizing a small "crash pad" to fall onto and a "spotter" for safety. Climbers do "boulder problems," where the solution is deciphering and executing a series of moves to complete the problem.

bridging: *See stemming.*

bucket: A handhold large enough to fully latch onto, like the handle of a bucket; also called a "jug."

buttress: An outside edge of rock that's much broader than an arête.

cam: Short for "spring-loaded camming device"; also refers to the single lobe or cam or camming device; also a verb used to describe the act of counterforce wherein a downward and outward force is created against the walls of a crack.

Camalot: Brand name for a type of spring-loaded camming device (SLCD) manufactured by Black Diamond Equipment. The Camalot was the first SLCD with two axles, which affords a greater range of placement for a given size.

camming device: Common term for a spring-loaded camming device (SLCD).

campus: To climb an overhanging section of rock using the arms only; a method of training grip, contact, and upper body strength.

carabiner: A high-strength aluminum alloy ring equipped with a spring-loaded snap gate; sometimes called "biners."

CE: Certified for Europe.

ceiling: A section of rock that extends out above your head; an overhang of sufficient size to loom overhead; sometimes called roof.

chalk: Carbonate of magnesium powder carried in a small "chalk bag," used to prevent fingers and hands from sweating and to provide a firmer grip in warm conditions.

chalk bag: A small bag filled with chalk and carried on a belt around a climber's waist.

chickenhead: A bulbous knob of rock.

chimney: A crack of sufficient size to accept an entire body.

chock: *See nut.*

chockstone: A rock lodged in a crack.

choss, chossy: Dirty, loose, rotten, and otherwise unappealing rock.

Class 1: Mountain travel classification for walking on relatively flat ground and trail hiking.

Class 2: Mountain travel classification for hiking over rough ground, such as scree and talus; may require the use of hands for stability.

Class 3: Mountain travel classification for scrambling that requires the use of hands and careful foot placement.

Class 4: Mountain travel classification for scrambling over steep and exposed terrain; a rope may be required for safety on exposed areas.

Class 5: Mountain travel classification for technical "free" climbing where terrain is steep and exposed, requiring the use of ropes, protection hardware, and related techniques; *see Yosemite Decimal System (YDS)*.

Class 6: Mountain travel classification for aid climbing where climbing equipment is used for balance, rest, or progress; denoted with a capital "A" followed by numerals 0 to 5 (e.g., 5.9/A3 means the free climbing difficulties are up to 5.9 with an aid section of A3 difficulty).

clean: Routes that are mostly free of vegetation or loose rock, or where you don't need to place pitons; also the act of removing chocks and other gear from a pitch.

clean climbing: Climbing that requires only removable protection; no pitons necessary.

cleaning tool: A metal pick used to poke and pry nuts from a crack; also known as a "nut tool."

cliff: A high, steep, or overhanging face of rock.

clove hitch: A secure and adjustable hitch used to attach a rope to a carabiner.

cold shuts: Metal hooks commonly found in pairs as anchors atop short sport climbs to facilitate lowering off; can be open, with gates, or welded shut.

cordelette: A short length of cord, normally 18 to 25 feet in length, often tied into a loop, used to equalize multiple anchor points. For nylon cord, 7mm is the standard diameter. High-strength (Technora or Spectra) cord is often used in 5mm or 6mm diameter.

crack: A fissure in the rock varying from extremely thin and narrow to as wide as a chimney.

crag: Another name for a cliff or rock formation.

crash pad: A portable foam pad used in bouldering.

crimp: A hand grip where the first knuckle is extended and the second knuckle is flexed, allowing the fingertips to rest on a small ledge.

crimps: Small but positive sharp edges.

crux: The most difficult move or sequence of moves on a climb, typically marked on topos with the difficulty rating.

dihedral: An inside corner of the climbing surface, formed by two planes of rock, like the angle formed by the pages of an open book; also called an "open book."

direct belay: To belay directly off the anchor.

downclimb: A descent without rope, usually when rappelling is unsafe or impractical.

drag: The resistance of the rope running through carabiners; commonly referred to as "rope drag."

dynamic rope: A climbing rope with built-in stretch to absorb the energy of a fall, typically around 9 percent stretch under body weight and up to 35 percent in a big fall.

dyno: A dynamic move or explosive leap for a hold otherwise out of reach.

edge: A small hold, or the act of standing on an edge.

edging: Using the very edge of the shoe on any clear-cut hold.

EN: European Norm.

equalette: An anchor-rigging technique using a cordelette, tied by forming a U shape with the cordelette, then tying two overhand knots at the center point, about 12 inches apart. A carabiner is clipped into each loop of cord between the knots to create a self-equalizing rig with minimal extension. The four strands, or "arms," of the cordelette can be attached to various anchors.

exposure: A relative situation where a climb has particularly noticeable sheerness.

extension: The potential for an anchor system's slings or cord to lengthen if one piece in the anchor system fails, causing a higher force on the remaining anchor or anchors.

fall factor: An equation that calculates the severity of a fall: the total distance of the fall divided by the length of rope from the belay.

finger crack: A crack climbed by wedging and jamming the fingers into the crack.

finger jams: Wedging the fingers into constrictions in a crack.

fireman's belay: A technique used to belay a rappelling climber by pulling down on the rope below the rappeller, creating tension that stops the rappeller from further movement down the rope.

first free ascent: The first free climb of a route previously climbed by aid climbing.

fist jam: Placing and wedging a fist sideways in a crack with the fingers curled inward toward the palm, providing a secure enough jam to pull on.

fixed anchor: Any permanent anchor left for all climbers to utilize, typically bolts or pitons.

flag: A climbing technique using a limb as a counterbalance.

flakes: A wafer or section of rock where a crack runs parallel to the plane of the main rock structure, as opposed to a "straight-in" crack that runs perpendicular to the plane of the main rock face.

flaking a rope: Uncoiling a rope into a loose pile, with one end on the bottom and the other end on the top of the pile; also called "stacking" a rope.

flared crack: Any crack that increases in dimension either inward or outward.

flash: Free climbing a route from bottom to top on your first try, without falling or hanging on the rope.

footwork: The art and method of standing on holds.

free: *See free climb.*

free ascent: *See free climb.*

free climb: The upward progress gained by a climber's own efforts, using hands, feet, and any part of the body on available features, unaided or free of attending ropes and gear. Rope is used only to safeguard against injury, not for upward progress or resting. Opposite of aid climb; also called "free" or "free ascent."

free solo: Free climbing a route without the use of a rope.

friction hitch: One of several hitches tied around a rope using a piece of smaller cord or a sling, which grips when weight is applied but can be loosened and slid up the rope when not under tension; commonly used to ascend a rope and in self-rescue techniques.

Friend: The name of the original spring-loaded camming device (SLCD) designed by Ray Jardine and marketed by the Wild Country Company in 1977. The word "friend" became a generic term for any SLCD.

frog step: Bringing one foot up, then the other, while keeping your torso at the same level, forming a crouched, or "bullfrog," position.

gaston: To grip handholds with the hands in a thumbs-down position, then pull outward, like prying apart elevator doors. Can also be one hand in the thumbs-down position on a handhold above and to the side of the body.

girth-hitch: A hitch used to connect webbing or cord around a feature to create an anchor by looping around the object then back through the sling or cord.

gobies: Hand abrasions.

Grade: A rating that tells how much time an experienced climber will take on a given climb, referring to the level of commitment required by the average climbing team; denoted by Roman numerals.

Grade I: A climb that may take only a few hours to complete.

Grade II: A climb that may take 3 to 4 hours.

Grade III: A climb that may take 4 to 6 hours, typically done in half a day.

Grade IV: A climb that may take a full day.

Grade V: A climb that normally takes two days, requiring a bivouac.

Grade VI: A climb that normally takes two or more days on the wall, requiring several bivouacs by the average party.

Grigri: A belay device with assisted braking, manufactured by Petzl.

gripped: Extremely scared.

ground anchor: An anchor used to secure a belayer at the base of a climb.

hangdog, hangdogging: Hanging on the rope to rest; not a free ascent. Sport climbers will often "hangdog" up a route to practice the moves and prepare for a later "free" ascent.

headwall: A much steeper section of cliff, found toward the top.

heel hooking: Hooking the heel on a large hold on overhanging rock above your head and pulling with the leg much like a third arm.

hex, hexes: *See hexentric.*

hexentric: A six-sided chock made by Black Diamond Equipment that can be wedged into cracks; commonly called a "hex."

highball: A term used to describe a bouldering problem that is high off the ground.

hip belay: To belay by wrapping the rope around your waist to create friction.

horn: A generally small, knoblike projection of rock.

indirect belay: To belay from the harness, not directly off the anchor.

jam: Wedging feet, hands, fingers, or other body parts to gain purchase in a crack.

Joshua Tree System: A rigging technique for toproping using an extension rope and a V configuration to create a master point over the edge of the cliff.

jug: A handhold shaped like a jug handle.

jumar: Term commonly used to refer to a device used to ascend a climbing rope; also a verb (i.e., "jumaring" the rope means ascending the rope).

killer: Extraordinarily good.

latch: To successfully grip a hold.

layback: Climbing maneuver that entails pulling with the hands while pushing with the feet; also called "lieback."

laybacking: *See layback.*

lead: To be the first on a climb, belayed from below, and placing protection to safeguard against a fall.

lieback: Climbing maneuver that entails pulling with the hands while pushing with the feet; also called "layback."

liebacking: *See lieback.*

line: The path of the route, usually the line of least resistance between other major features of the rock.

lock-off: Hanging by one arm on a single handhold with enough strength to allow the other hand to release its grip and move up to a new handhold.

loop strength: The minimum breaking strength of a sling or cord when tested in a single, continuous loop; like a Dyneema sewn into a loop with bartacked stitching or a cord tied into a loop with a knot.

lunge: An out-of-control dynamic move, a jump for a far-off hold.

magic X: *See sliding X.*

manky: Of poor quality, as in "a manky finger jam" or "manky protection placement."

mantle: A series of climbing moves enabling you to grab a feature (like a ledge) and maneuver up to where you're standing on it, usually accomplished by pulling up then pressing down with one or both palms while bringing up one foot (similar to getting out of the deep end of a swimming pool).

mantleshelf: A rock feature, typically a ledge with scant holds directly above.

mantling: The act of surmounting a mantleshelf.

master point (aka power point): The equalized point in an anchor system; the point a climber clips into.

micro-nut: A very small nut used mainly for aid climbing.

mountaineering: Reaching mountaintops using a combination of skills (such as rock climbing and ice climbing), usually involving varying degrees of objective hazards.

move: One of a series of motions necessary to gain climbing distance.

multipitch: A route with multiple belay stations (rope lengths).

Munter hitch: A hitch used for belaying that requires no gear other than a carabiner.

natural anchor: An anchor made from a feature occurring in nature, such as a chockstone, rock tunnel, horn, tree, boulder, etc.

nut: A wedged-shaped piece of metal designed to be used as an anchor in a crack; also called a "chock."

nut tool: A metal pick used to tap and pry nuts to facilitate removal or "cleaning."

off-width: A crack that is too wide to use as a finger, hand, or fist jam but too narrow to get inside and climb as a chimney.

on-sight: To successfully climb a route without prior knowledge or experience of the moves.

opposition: Nuts, anchors, or climbing maneuvers that are held in place by the simultaneous stress of two forces working against each other.

overhang, overhanging: A section of rock that is steeper than vertical.

peg: *See piton.*

pinch grip: A handhold where the thumb pinches in opposition to the fingers on either side of a projection.

pinkpoint: To lead (without falling) a climb that has been pre-protected with gear and rigged with quickdraws.

pins: *See pitons.*

pin scar: A mark of damage left in a crack by repeated placement and removal of pitons.

pitch: The distance between belays.

pitons: Metal spikes of various shapes that are hammered into the rock to provide anchors in cracks; sometimes called "pins" or "pegs." These types of anchors were common up to the 1970s but are rarely used today.

power point: *See master point.*

pre-equalized: Tying off an anchor system for an anticipated force in only one direction.

pro: *See protection.*

protection: The anchors used to safeguard the leader; sometimes called "pro." Until the 1970s, protection devices were almost exclusively pitons—steel spikes that were hammered into cracks in the rock. Since then, various nuts and camming devices have virtually replaced pitons as protection devices. These chocks and cams are fitted into cracks, and the rope is attached to them. In the absence of cracks, permanent bolt anchors are installed into the rock. The leader clips into the protection and proceeds to climb past it. If the leader falls, he or she will travel at least twice the distance from above the last point of protection (rope stretch adds more distance).

prusik: Both the knot and any means by which you mechanically ascend a rope.

quad: A rigging technique accomplished by doubling a cordelette and clipping it to two anchor points, quadrupling the strands. Two overhand knots are tied in the four strands, and carabiners are clipped to three of the four strands between the knots, creating a self-equalizing anchor system with minimal extension.

quickdraws: Short slings with carabiners at both ends that help provide drag-free rope management for the leader.

quick link: An aluminum or steel screw link often found on rappel anchors, mostly bought from hardware stores, although some manufacturers make CE-certified quick links for climbing (like the Petzl maillon rapide).

rack: The collection of gear a climber takes up the climb.

rappel: To descend by sliding down a rope, typically utilizing a mechanical braking device.

rapping: Informal term for rappelling.

redpoint: To lead a route from bottom to top in one push, clipping protection as you go, without falling or resting on protection.

redirected belay: To belay by running the rope through a belay device attached to the harness then back through an anchor.

RENE: Acronym for Redundancy, Equalization, and No Extension.

Rocks: Brand name for a line of passive nuts developed by Mark Valance and sold by Wild Country.

roof: A section of rock that extends out above your head; sometimes called a ceiling.

rope direct belay: To belay from an extended master point using the climbing rope.

R-rated climbs: Protection or danger rating for climbs with serious injury potential; protection may be sparse or "runout," or some placements may not hold a fall.

runner: *See sling.*

runout: The distance between two points of protection; often refers to a long stretch of climbing without protection.

sandbagging: The "shameful" practice of a first ascent team underrating the actual difficulty of a given route.

second: The second person on a rope team, usually the leader's belayer.

self-equalizing: An anchor system that adjusts to withstand a force in multiple directions.

"Send it": An emphatic statement to someone encouraging him or her to hang in and finish a route without falling.

sharp end: The lead climber's end of the rope.

shelf: The pre-equalized point on a cordelette directly above the master point knot; all loops must be clipped for redundancy.

shred: To do really well; to dominate.

sidepull: Pulling on a vertically aligned hold to the side of the body.

signals: A set of commands used between climber and belayer.

slab: A less than vertical, or low-angle, section of a rock face.

SLCD (spring-loaded camming device): *See Friend.*

sliding X (aka magic X): A self-equalizing sling rigged between two anchor points.

sling: Webbing sewn or tied into a loop; also called a runner.

smear, smearing: Standing on a sloping foothold and utilizing friction in order to adhere to the rock.

"soft" ratings: Ratings deemed harder than the actual difficulty of a given route.

sport climbing: Similar to traditional rock climbing but with protection and anchors (bolts) already in place. Instead of using nuts and cams, the climber uses quickdraws, clipping bolts for protection. Most sport climbing is face climbing and is usually only one pitch in length, but it can be multi-pitch. With the danger element removed, the emphasis is on technique and doing hard moves.

spotter: A person designated to slow the fall of a boulderer, especially to keep the boulderer's head from hitting the ground.

spring-loaded camming device (SLCD): *See Friend.*

stance: A standing rest spot, often the site of a belay.

static rope: A rope with virtually no stretch.

stem, stemming: The process of counterpressuring with the feet between two widely spaced holds; also called "bridging."

stopper knot: A safety knot tied on the end of a rope to prevent accidents.

Stoppers: Brand name for one of the original (and now one of the most commonly used) wedge-shaped tapered nut designs, sold by Black Diamond Equipment.

sustained: Climbing adjective that indicates the continuous nature of the climb.

tail: The length of the end of a rope protruding from a knot.

TCU (three-cam unit): A type of spring-loaded camming device (SLCD) with just three cams instead of four.

tensile strength: The minimum breaking strength of a sling, cord, or rope when tested on a single strand.

thin: A climb or hold of relatively featureless character.

thread: A sling or cord looped through a tunnel in the rock structure.

topo: A detailed diagram showing a climbing route up a cliff.

toprope: A belay from an anchor point above that protects the climber from falling even a short distance.

toproping: *See toprope.*

trad: *See traditional rock climbing.*

traditional rock climbing: Climbing a route where the leader places gear (nuts and cams) for protection and anchors, to be removed later by the second, or "follower"; as opposed to sport climbing, which relies solely on bolts for protection and anchors; also called "trad climbing."

traverse: To move sideways, without altitude gain.

Tricam: A mechanical wedge that acts as both a nut and a cam.

tweak: To injure, as in "a tweaked finger tendon."

UIAA: Union Internationale des Associations d'Alpinisme.

undercling: Grabbing a hold (usually a flake) with the palm up and fingers underneath the hold, then pulling outward with the arm while pushing against the rock with the feet, much like a lieback.

V system: The universal bouldering language, established in the early 1990s at Hueco Tanks, Texas. Ratings range from V0 to V16, with V0 being the easiest and V15 being roughly equivalent to 5.15b YDS.

vector: A measurement of force and direction in anchor systems.

wall: A long climb traditionally done over multiple days, but which may take just a few hours for ace climbers; *see big wall.*

water knot: A knot used to tie a loop of webbing.

webbing: Synthetic fiber woven flat like a strap, used to make slings. Nylon webbing was used exclusively for slings up to the 1990s; now slings are also made from Spectra and Dyneema webbing.

wired: Known well, as in "a wired route."

work, worked, or working: To practice the moves of a difficult route via toprope or hangdogging.

X-rated climbs: Protection or danger rating for climbs with groundfall and death potential.

YDS: *See Yosemite Decimal System.*

Yosemite Decimal System (YDS): The American grading scale for identifying technical difficulty of routes, where 5 denotes the class and the numerals following the decimal point indicate the difficulty rating (5.0 to 5.15), usually according to the most difficult move. Subgrades (a, b, c, and d) are used on climbs rated 5.10 and harder.

Z system: A raising system that uses a 3:1 mechanical advantage.

Index

nuts and, 80–81, 86
pitons and, 98–99
rockfall, 222
Rock Wise (Ament), 222
rope
    backpacker (butterfly) coil,
        16–21
    care and use of, 15
    closing the system, 223–24
    marking middle of, 16, 208
    mountaineer's coil, 22
    New England coil, 23–24
    retrieving, 208–9
    tossing, 205–6
    types, 13–14, 208
    uncoiling for first time, 16
    See also Hitches; Knots; Loops
rope direct belay, 187–88
rubric for anchor system
    evaluation, 123–25, 133

safety checks
    ABC check, 178, 179, 180, 182,
        224
    ABCDE checklist, 201
    BARCK check, 224
    rappelling checks, 201, 203
    standard climbing signals,
        172–73
    See also Risk management
Safety Pro rope, 13
Salathe, John, 78
screwgate locking carabiner, 32–33
self-equalizing anchor
    defined, 107
    equalette, 120
    quad, 118–19
    sliding X, 113–17
semi-static rope. *See* Low-stretch
    rope
shoes, 5, 10–11, 51
    See also Smearing technique

sidepull combinations, 37
site selection, 1
SLCD. *See* Spring-loaded
    camming device (SLCD)
sliding X system, 113–17, 128
slings
    Dyneema slings, 26–28, 108,
        125–28
    nylon, 25–28, 125–28, 199, 222
    Spectra, 26–27, 125–28
slip hitch, 75
SMC company, 100–101, 102
smearing technique, 38, 40
SOS principle, 123
Spectra slings, 26–27, 125–28
spinner bolt, 103, 104
sport climbing, 7
spring-loaded camming device
    (SLCD)
    about, 87–88
    invention of, 86–89
    need for instruction in use of,
        96–98
    placement of, 89–98
squeeze chimney, 61–62
SRENE principle, 107, 123, 133
stance
    for belaying, 175–76
    for rappelling, 196, 197
static rope, 13, 14, 26
steep face climbing
    about, 41–42
    crack climbing comparison, 51
    deadpoint principle, 46–47
    face holds, 42–43
    hip positions, 43–44
    mantles, 47–49
    push/pull technique, 44–46
    slab climbing, 37–41
stemming, 62, 64
Sterling Chain Reactor, 199, 200,
    204

Sterling Rope uncoiling method,
    16
sticky rubber shoes, 37
Stonemasters, 37
stopper knot, 166–67, 200
Stopper nut, 81–83, 123
swami belts, 9

Tahquitz Rock, 4–6
tape for hands, 65–67
TCUs (three-cam units), 89
teaching rock climbing. *See*
    Instruction in rock climbing
tell/show/do principle, 213, 214,
    217
tensile strength, 27
tethers, 132–35, 199
thin hand jam, 54, 55
"third hand" hitch, 160
threads in rock, 73, 76
three-cam units (TCUs), 89
3:1 raising system, 185–86
thumb-down/thumb-up positions,
    52–53
topos, 1
toproping
    benefits, ix
    defined, 6
    guidebooks, 1–2
    racks for, 98
    ratings of cliffs, 1–6
    site selection, 1
    transitioning to rappelling from,
        207–8
    typical day of, 2–4
traditional climbing, 7
Trango Cinch, 171
trees as anchors, 73–74, 76, 141–
    42, 197
triangular configuration, 121
tri-axial loading, 33
Tricams, 79–82

About the Author

Bob Gaines began rock climbing at Joshua Tree National Park in the 1970s. Since then he has pioneered more than 500 first ascents in the park.

Bob began his career as a professional rock climbing guide in 1983 and is an American Mountain Guides Association Certified Rock Instructor. He is the coauthor of *Rock Climbing: The AMGA Single Pitch Manual*, the textbook for the AMGA's single-pitch instructor program.

Bob has worked extensively in the film business as a climbing stunt coordinator. He has coordinated more than forty television commercials and was Sylvester Stallone's climbing instructor for the movie *Cliffhanger*. Bob doubled for William Shatner in *Star Trek V: The Final Frontier* as Captain Kirk free soloing on El Capitan in Yosemite.

Bob has worked extensively training US military special forces, including the elite US Navy SEAL Team 6, and is known for his technical expertise in anchoring and rescue techniques.

He is also the author of *Best Climbs Joshua Tree National Park, Best Climbs Tahquitz and Suicide Rocks, Rappelling*, and *Advanced Rock Climbing* and is coauthor of *Climbing Anchors* and the *Climbing Anchors Field Guide* (with John Long).

Bob's other passion is fly fishing. He currently holds thirteen International Game Fish Association world records.